The Poshmark Guide for Individuals and Small Businesses:

How We Achieved a Five-Figure Revenue Stream
Within Our First Year

By

John Lim

DEDICATION

For Mom and Dad, the bravest and most intrepid small business owners I've ever known. You embody the American Dream to its fullest and are a shining light for others to follow.

CONTENTS

ACKNOWLEDGMENTS

Thank you to my brilliant editor, Megan Prikhodko. Your tireless efforts, eagle-eye for detail, and critical feedback helped me find the right words to say exactly what needed to be said. Thank you for putting up with my never-ending stream of Gantt chart jokes. Every writer should have a "Megan" in their lives. We would end up with far better books on our shelves if we did.

Thank you, Manish Chandra, Nyzelle Ornedo-Ibarra, Ashley Ortiz, Sera Michael, Camille Forde, Adiel Nuesmeyer, and to so many wonderful people at Poshmark for your guidance, support, and feedback during the writing process. Additional thanks to Natasha Won, Serena Jew, Daria Mohazab, Jennifer Chen Tran, Angelo Spenillo, Jamie Seward, Elena Stokes, and The Johns Hopkins University Alumni Association.

To an amazing group of Poshmark friends ("PFFs"): Ashley Waters Gordon ("AWG") of @kensingtoncrew, Stefanie S. of @stefanies23, and Işıl ("Izzy") Pollack and Gül ("Rose") Gümüştaş of @izzyandrose, your time, feedback, and counsel were invaluable, and this book is that much richer for it. I've learned so much from each of you, and I'm grateful for your friendship. Reader, if you're looking to start on Poshmark, you would do well to follow these individuals who are crushing it each, and every day.

To my mom: I never imagined that I would get to help Dad continue building the business you started. Your love, guidance, and spirit are a daily reminder to keep putting my best foot forward. I love you and miss you, always.

Finally, to my dad: you are the most forward-thinking person I know. Each time you get that spark I somehow end up on a wild ride that takes me on a magnificent journey like this one. I'm proud to be your son, beyond what I can sum up in a few sentences. I love you.

INTRODUCTION

Let me start this book with a confession that may come as a shock. I hate shopping for clothes. I'm the type of guy who wears the same basic outfit of jeans, a t-shirt, non-descript but comfortable walking shoes, and on cold days, a sweater, peacoat, and cap. So, it may surprise you that in less than a year, I managed to build a five-figure business selling clothes; everything from designer high-heeled shoes to wedding gowns. While I'm not an expert in clothes, I've had a lengthy career in consulting; understanding what customers and clients are looking for, and finding solutions to problems, which is the cornerstone for most businesses. I also host a podcast called Moving Forward, which has given me the opportunity to speak with many entrepreneurs. All of these past experiences contributed to my success on Poshmark.

I fell into this world quite by accident, and because I have a dad who isn't shy about asking me to find solutions to big problems. My dad, Hyi ("Hi") Lim, is one of the gutsiest and scrappiest entrepreneurs I know. He came to this country in 1970 from Seoul, South Korea, with less than $200 in his pocket and limited English. Though he never got a formal education past high school, he has enough raw grit and life experience to fill three PhDs. He and my late mom built up a successful small clothing business located in the heart of Pikesville, Maryland. While many small shops came and went, they survived and thrived by selling high-end garments with red carpet level customer service. When my mom passed away in 2008, my dad turned to teaching sewing classes. He even launched a YouTube channel showcasing some of his tried-and-true industry secrets. His tutorial on hemming blue jeans is

1

currently within the top three ranked videos in the world on that topic with over 2M views. He regularly gets comments and praise from fans all over the world. In 2014, he entered into a partnership with his now second wife, a successful entrepreneur in the wedding and prom business. Together, they built up a successful boutique catering to brides and prom goers. Business was booming until 2016, when my dad noticed a growing and distressing trend. Customers would come in, browse, snap photos, and search for the same item on Amazon. Amazon was a looming 800 lb. gorilla and we had to find a way to adapt into this ever-changing consumer landscape. Over the next several years, we tried everything from eBay to Amazon FBA to Shopify. None of these proved to be the "silver bullet." Then, one fateful day in May 2018, I stumbled onto a platform called Poshmark. A few years prior, I had read a Buzzfeed article or two about it but didn't think this quirky app that catered to people selling items out of their closets was for us. But at that point, I was desperate. We were spending several hundred dollars a month on Amazon FBA and Shopify subscriptions without great results. Worse, Amazon's policy of "no questions asked" returns meant that of the few sales we generated, more than half ended up returned to us. Since Poshmark had no upfront costs, we had nothing to lose. I downloaded the app, set up our store, and put up a few listings. While, I would like to say sales just "rained in," that wasn't the case. It took learning a new language and a culture of "social selling," combining it with my dad's superior customer service practices to gain traction. When we finally did, it was our "aha moment." We landed our first sale in August of that year and from there, managed to generate five-figures by year's end.

I documented my Poshmark journey in 2019 on my podcast and currently, those episodes are among the most listened to. I've received comments on social media from individuals who have been inspired to start selling on the platform. Their enthusiasm and curiosity are part of the reason why I decided to write this book.

The other reason is that small businesses are suffering. The recent pandemic has obliterated thousands of local retail or "mom-and-pop" businesses. Throughout 2020 and into 2021, while headlines focused on large retailer bankruptcies, small businesses were not counted in those stats. Most simply closed their doors; crushed by a mix of sagging in-person sales, and state and local mandates, which forced them to limit hours, and navigate tricky, often polarizing mask mandates. Nationally, it is estimated that 100,000 small businesses shut down during the height of the pandemic with over 235 closing shop in our backyard, within the DC metro area.[1] While large chains like Target, Walmart, and Nordstrom were able to pivot to online sales, many small businesses struggled to make that transition due to costs, a steep learning curve, and a lack of clear guidance.[2] According to a 2020 McKinsey report, the aforementioned practices of social distancing, contactless payments, and online shopping have permanently shaped consumer habits, and will remain a lasting legacy as we exit the pandemic.[3] However, the report cautions that simply shifting sales online will not be enough, noting:

> [D]eclines in purchase intent of 70 to 80 percent in offline and 30 to 40 percent in online in Europe and North America, even in countries that haven't been under full lockdown. E-commerce is clearly not offsetting the sales declines in stores. Nevertheless, it has been a lifeline for fashion brands as stores have been shuttered—and it will continue to be critical during and after the recovery period.

This book is a deep dive into building an online business with the Poshmark platform and is aimed at two audiences: 1) individuals who wants to start a side hustle making some extra money, and 2) small retail clothing businesses that need to expand online. I'm proof positive that if I can do it, anyone can. Whether you're trying to expand an existing business online or simply clean out your closet, I'm going to share every secret and tactic I've learned to generate high sales with five-star ratings and glowing reviews.

I'll also cover some marketing and negotiating hacks that I've developed, which will help you stand out. Want to know how to sell items you haven't even listed? How do you run a holiday sale? And how do you handle customer complaints? I'll answer all these questions with real-life examples from our own experience. In the later chapters, I'll share how to take your business to the next level once you're ready to scale up.

Before we begin, I must provide some important disclaimers. This is not easy. Building a business that generates consistent sales takes time, effort, and a lot of hard work. Today, Poshmark is crowded with new sellers appearing every day. By the time you buy this book, there will probably be at least a hundred, if not more, sellers that have just set up their virtual storefronts. However, I'm going to challenge you to see this as a strength of the platform rather than an obstacle. There's a unique community and crowd sourcing aspect to Poshmark that will help you gain customers and sales. Speaking of sales, they don't always come immediately. I've seen people posting on Facebook or Twitter that they've listed items and haven't generated any sales. My hope is that you'll crush it within the first hour but don't be discouraged if it takes a few weeks or even months to gain any traction. Building a business is hard but if you're willing to put in the effort then this can be a rewarding side hustle, hobby, or even fulltime business.

This book is structured into three parts, each containing a series of chapters. In each chapter, I explore the principles and mechanics of the Poshmark platform. In part I, I cover getting started, including the process that led me to select Poshmark as our go-to online retail solution and why I think it's the best platform out there today for selling clothes. In part II, I explain transactions, negotiation strategies and tactics, interactions with customers, and troubleshooting problems. Part III is where you will learn how to level up as you grow your business with best practices for inventory management, marketing, and selling high-end items. Finally, we'll look at expanding your business by sourcing items wholesale.

Please note, most of the photos and illustrations include real examples from our Poshmark store with actual names and order numbers redacted and replaced with fake ones for privacy reasons. At the end of each chapter, you'll find best practice tips, and exercises.

The appendix at the very end of the book includes a quick reference checklist and two worksheets, one for inventory management and another for negotiating with customers. You'll also find all of the exercises together in case you prefer to read the book first as opposed to doing the exercises chapter-by-chapter.

Selling on Poshmark can and should be a rewarding and fun experience. For individual sellers, it can be a great way to earn some extra cash or start a business with low overhead costs by tapping into inventory you have in your closet. For retail businesses, selling online is no longer just a competitive advantage. Today, it's necessary to adapt, survive, and hopefully thrive, as evolving practices and habits have forever changed the way we do everyday tasks like shop for clothes.

Whatever your goals are, let's make them happen and move forward.

PART I

1 PLATFORM OVERWHELM

My dad who I mentioned in the introduction has been an entrepreneur for over 50 years. He's still going strong and, God bless him, I don't know how he does it. He comes from that generation of pioneers that see hard work as "retirement." He's an amazing guy who learned how to sew as a teenager and worked his way to become a head designer at London Fog, where he designed raincoats for over two decades.

Today, he and his business partner run a clothing shop with two locations. The stores cater to brides and bridesmaids for weddings, and high school teens for proms.

Business had been going extremely well until six years ago. In 2016, my dad noticed a growing trend. Customers would come into the shop, try on a bunch of outfits, and ultimately buy the items online. Amazon has not only changed the way we shop, but the way we approach in-store visits. I'm guilty of this. Every time, I contemplate buying something at a store, I open the Amazon app and scan the barcode to see if I can find it cheaper there. It's become second nature.

This growing trend has made business tougher for my dad. I listened to him as he shared the struggles of a small brick and mortar business owner and although I knew nothing about clothes, I had some experience selling on Amazon. During business school, I would sell all my textbooks at the end of each semester on the platform. I did well, selling them at cost or sometimes for a profit. Later, I dipped a toe in the water, selling private label health and beauty products through its Fulfilled by Amazon (FBA) program. I've also written and published a popular adult coloring book that's printed, distributed, sold, and marketed through Amazon's KDP self-publishing platform.

Given my experiences with selling on online, and as a consumer, I knew that we should explore ecommerce as a sales channel for my dad's business. Up until that point, he wasn't aware this was even possible.

We started with the aforementioned Amazon FBA program. We had two goals in mind. First, leverage online sales to alleviate sagging in-person purchases. Second, expand the business to reach larger markets, beyond his geographic limitations.

We spent several months creating a sales channel on Amazon. The key word being "months." The set-up was a maze of hurdles and in the end, we sold about six or seven dresses with more than half returned due to Amazon's "no questions asked" return policy. While I love Amazon as an individual consumer, it wasn't a good fit for my dad's business.

Next, we tried Shopify. I know several people who love Shopify and have had great success with it. After doing a little homework, we decided to give it a shot. This was early 2018. While it was easier than Amazon, it wasn't a great fit for selling clothes of different sizes and varieties. In the end, we spent six months on Shopify and didn't make a sale. I'll cover these and other platforms more in depth later in the book.

What now? We had been chasing the "take your business online" dream for a year and a half and it seemed further away with increasing hoops to jump through. It was now May 2018, and we were spinning our wheels, focusing more on learning these platforms and overcoming multiple obstacles than on sales. In a moment of frustration, I took a break and Googled "sites to sell clothes on" and came across Poshmark.

EXERCISE: In one or two sentences, write out your goal(s) for selling online. Specify why you want to sell clothes online. Are you doing this to clear out your closet or develop a business or side hustle? Where do you see your business or venture in six months or one year.

_____

_____

_____

_____

_____

2 GETTING STARTED ON POSHMARK

In the last chapter, I talked about the year and a half journey (struggle) to help my dad take his retail business online, including pain points we experienced on Amazon and Shopify. In a moment of sheer desperation, I stumbled onto Poshmark.

I had read a few articles about Poshmark in the past but hadn't paid much attention to it since it was designed for individuals who wanted to sell clothes from their closets online. However, by this point I was desperate for a solution. I took a deeper dive and discovered that Poshmark is primarily a mobile platform. It has a website but every part of the business, from listing to communications to closing sales can be done right on your phone. The mobile-first approach appealed to me greatly as it was something I struggled with on the other platforms. For Amazon and Shopify, most of the heavy lifting required me to be in front of a desktop. This proved time consuming, especially when it came to updating listings or creating new ones on the fly. With cautious optimism, I downloaded the Poshmark app. It was May 2018, and I was stuck on a html coding issue on Shopify. I was equal parts frustrated and desperate. I figured we had nothing to lose in trying out the app.

The first thing I discovered about Poshmark is that there are no upfront costs or fees. Unlike Amazon pro or Shopify, all the costs are deducted from sales. For small ticket, low-priced items, Poshmark takes a flat fee. For items above a certain amount, Poshmark charges 20%. If that seems high, keep in mind that eBay and Amazon also charge commissions in addition to subscription fees for their pro plans. While Shopify's post-sales fees were lower than Amazon's, we had to pay a monthly subscription fee, regardless of sales.

Setup on the Poshmark app was a breeze. It was the first ecommerce platform that I came across that was truly "out of the box."

We started with branding my dad's store. Your store's branding is your first impression as a Poshmark seller. Once you download the app, look at different Poshmark sellers. The ones that use generic circles for avatars and blank backgrounds blend together and get lost in the shuffle. The ones that invest the time into their branding stand out in a crowded marketplace.

Figure 2.1 Blank profile header.

Figure 2.2 Our profile header.

After setting up our account, I listed our first items, averaging two to five minutes per item, which included the following steps:

- Snap photos of the item from my phone. Poshmark allows 16 photos per item.
- Fill in the blanks on the item:
    o Title: short description with basic info.
    o Description: longer, expanded with greater detail.

- o   Use the menus to designate classification, type, size, condition, color, etc.
- o   Set your price: Poshmark will show you a preview of how much you will make after fees.
- o   Publish the item.

[Note: the time doesn't include setting up clothes on mannequins. This will add an extra 2-5 minutes depending on the garment.]

We'll cover the listing steps in greater detail over the next chapters, adding nuances and best practices to make your listings stand out.

- ● **BEST PRACTICE TIP:** Take a panoramic photo from your phone for your header image (see Figure 2.2 for an example).

- ● **EXERCISE:** Dig into Poshmark: feel free to research articles like I did (good and bad, pros and cons) and read through Poshmark's website. Check out the fee structure. Remember, Poshmark doesn't charge a setup or listing fee and takes its commission post-sales. Next, download the Poshmark app and set up your account. Spend time on branding your store. (Estimated time: 10 minutes):
  - o   Download the app and set up your store.
  - o   Give it a name and handle (Poshmark user ID): come up with something that's easy such as your initials, a play on your name or, if you're a business, a username that matches your brand.
  - o   Fill in some basic info.
  - o   Upload a header and bio photo.

If you're feeling adventurous, list your first item. We'll go over the process in more detail in the next chapters so you can also wait if you're not quite ready for that.

3 LISTING BASICS

Building off the last chapter, let's do a deep dive into creating a Poshmark listing with some tried and proven best practices. By now, you should have set up your Poshmark account and branded it accordingly. With that complete, let's turn our attention to listing basics.

Below is the most powerful button on the app; one you should get well acquainted with.

Here is a high-level list of what you'll need to create a listing:

- **Photos:** Poshmark allows you to upload up to sixteen photos per item. Make use of these. I recommend using at least eight photos to showcase multiple angles of each item. Save a few photo slots in case you need to update a listing with additional details or to answer questions (more on this later).
- **Title:** create a simple but descriptive title (50-character limit).

- **Description:** here, you get a lot more space to fill in the details on your listing. Be robust with a fuller description, including brand name, fabric, measurements, etc.

Below the description field, you will see menus to fill in the rest of the details, including category and price. Let's take a closer look at each element of a listing.

Figure 3.1 Categories and sample listing.

Listing Elements

Element 1: Photos

The first and most important part of listings are photos. Poshmark allocates sixteen photos per listing. As mentioned, try to use at least eight photos to capture different angles of the item: front, side, and back. You don't need a lot of fancy equipment or lighting. Use your phone and take clear, clean photos that highlight the details of your item. I also recommend that you use a mannequin or model (yourself or a friend) as opposed to a hanger. Clothes on hangers look flat and unflattering. They simply can't reflect the full three-dimensional nuances of a garment. You want to showcase what the item will look like when worn.

Figure 3.2 Multiple angle photos of a Poshmark listing.

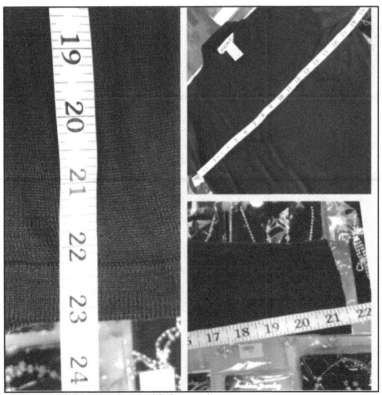

Figure 3.3 Sample photo grid showcasing measurements on a sweater.

Figure 3.4 Left-Right: sample size chart post and Poshmark size chart.

Figure 3.5 Example of a photo showcasing a flaw.

Element 2: Video

In 2021, Poshmark took a bold step by adding video to the platform. Poshmark sellers ("Poshers") can now post video "stories" up to 15 seconds in length and add one video to each listing. Video deserves its own chapter so I will cover it in greater detail later. We've incorporated videos for all of our newer listings, and it has made a huge difference. Somewhat surprisingly, and despite being a highly requested feature, many Poshers are still not taking advantage of it. Therefore, if you really want to stand out, add videos to give buyers a full 360 view of your garment. It's not hard and I'll share our secrets on creating professional looking videos that take less than five minutes.

Element 3: Title

After you snap photos of your listing, you will need to add a title. Poshmark only allows 50 characters so be economical with your verbiage, while making your titles descriptive. Don't just write "dress" or "jacket" but describe the item. For example, "Red prom dress with spaghetti straps and sequins" or "Striped golf shirt, worn once." You can also put the brand name in the title if you want to highlight it. I generally don't in favor of using the space for descriptive words. I leave the brand for the description field, and it is also a separate menu option.

Element 4: Description

Underneath the title, you have more real estate to add a fuller description. This is where you can add brand, color, fabric, more details, the condition of the item, including any flaws, and measurements. Some sellers will add a line of hashtags to increase an item's searchability. For example: #dress #prom #reddress #weddingdress #specialoccasion #<brand name>.

In addition to the basics, I recommend you add a SKU (stock keeping unit) code to your listings. Poshmark has a separate section at the bottom called "Additional Details (Private)" where you can add a SKU, and other details such as original price and notes. However, I find it faster to simply add the SKU as part of the description as it will save you an extra click. The SKU can be a style number from an item's tag, or you can create your own system. Use SKUs to keep track of your inventory. Even if you have a small closet, get into this practice early. If you grow your Poshmark store, you'll be that much more organized, and you'll thank me later.

For my dad's business, we now have over 1,500 listings. The SKU allows us to search for items quickly. This is extremely important for updating inventory if, as in the case of a retail business, you list an item that's available for sale in-store. If you sell a listing in-store, at a flea market, or donate it, you'll need to find it quickly so you can update the listing without having to scroll through hundreds of items. SKUs become part of your listing's search engine optimization or SEO. As of the writing of this book, Poshmark now allows you to search within your closet, which make SKUs an even more precise way to search for a specific item. More on this later.

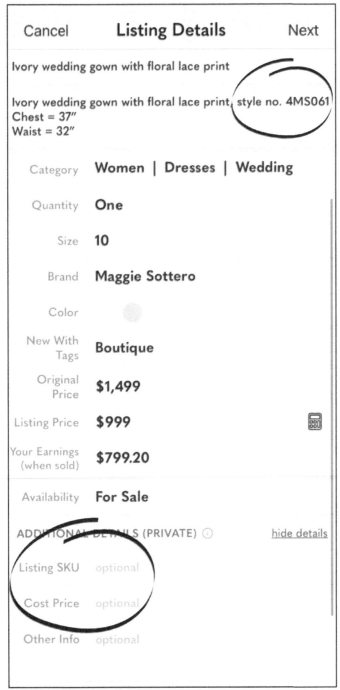

Figure 3.6 SKU and additional details section.

After you fill out the description, complete your listing with a series of menu items.

Element 5: Category

Categories range from general to specific, so it's important to identify what the item is and where it belongs. Start at the top category, and choose whether it's a garment for women, men, kids, a home good, pet good, or electronic item. From there choose a subcategory such as "dresses." Within dresses, you can subcategorize or choose "none" to leave it general. Try to be as specific as you can. There's a big difference between "wedding" and "prom" dresses. Using subcategories will allow potential buyers to find your item with greater ease and precision.

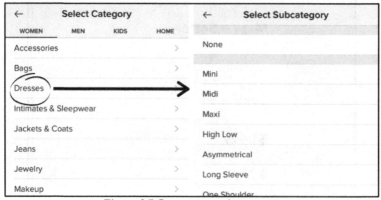

Figure 3.7 Category to subcategory.

Element 6: Quantity

If you are listing a single item, choose "One." If you have more than one in different sizes, choose "Multiple."

Element 7: Size

If you choose "Multiple" under quantity, you will see a menu of sizes depending on the item. For example, if you are listing a dress, you can choose "Standard," "Plus," "Petite," "Juniors," "Maternity," or "Custom." Within each category, you will see a list of sizes, both letter and numeric. If the size standard isn't there, choose "Custom" to create your own. This may be the case with certain European or other non-US size protocols. As you choose the size, for example size 12 or M, you will see an option to list quantity per size. Use these options to list inventory you have in stock.

This simple feature is one of my favorites that puts Poshmark head and shoulders above many of the other platforms we've tried.

Element 8: Brand

As mentioned above, brand name has its own field. As you type within this section, Poshmark will autosuggest brand names from its library of brand listings to select. If the brand is not available as a pre-select, you can type it out and add it to the listing. I also recommend adding the brand name to the description (in text or as a hashtag or both) to make it that much more discoverable.

Element 9: Color

Choose the color for the item. You can tag up to two basic colors per listing. For blends or unique colors, you may want to use a combination (e.g., for "ivory" or "off white," I might tag a combination of white and cream). Be sure to describe the exact color in the title or description fields. For similar items with different colors, create separate listings.

Element 10: New with Tags

This menu allows you to indicate the condition of the item you're listing. "New with tags" refers to new clothes bought off the rack that have never been worn and still have the original tags. Choose "No" for new items without tags or for used items. If you are running a retail store like my dad or selling items you've purchased directly from a wholesaler, there is a separate "Boutique" category you can use within "New." Boutique indicates items that were purchased from a supplier or wholesaler. We will cover "Boutique" listings and wholesale buying in a later chapter.

Element 11: Style tags

Underneath "New with Tags," you can add three "style tags," which provide additional details for your listing, including colors or fabrics. You can choose from a pre-set list or type in your own. Style tags are a recent addition that index listings, making them more discoverable to potential buyers.

Figure 3.8 Example of style tags, including two pre-set and one manually added.

Element 12: Original price

List the original price you paid for the item or in the case of "Boutique" items, the fair market value or in-store price of the item.

Element 13: Listing price

This is what you're willing to sell the item for. If you're open to negotiating price, use this as the baseline starting point. We'll cover negotiations in a separate chapter. For now, set a "Listing Price" which reflects a discount if you wish to offer one. You can also use the "Original Price" if you are trying to sell it for the same price. The price you set depends on your seller motivation. Some of you may simply want to clear out a closet full of clothes you no longer wear in exchange for cash. For others, you may be trying to make a profit off a new item, also known as "retail arbitrage." I recommend offering a discount, especially if it's NWT. As Poshmark is a marketplace where many sellers sell secondhand or used items, most buyers are looking for a discount. Even in the case of "Boutique" items, a discounted price will often have a healthy profit margin over the per unit cost from a wholesaler.

The "Listing Price" will display a calculation underneath of "your earnings"

24

if the item sells. This is how much you'll make net Poshmark's commission.

Once you fill out the fields, hit "Next" and you will be prompted to "List" the item, which will make it active on your store and available to buy or make an offer on. If you need to update a listing, simply click "Edit" to make changes, including description, quantity, and price.

Element 14: Availability

The availability field allows you to set the status of the listing. By default, all new listings will be "for sale," meaning they're available for purchase as soon as you publish the listing. You can set it to "not for sale," which means the listing will display but not be available for purchase. This is useful for administrative posts and for changing the status of items you no longer have in your inventory but wish to keep displayed. I'll go into detail on why you might want to do this in a later chapter.

Recently, Poshmark added a third option: drops, in which you set a month, day and time. This allows you to create a listing, have it appear in your closet but not yet be available to purchase until the "drops" date occurs. This is a great way to market items you plan to sell in the near future.

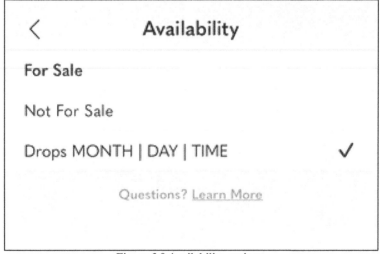

Figure 3.9 Availability options.

Element 15: Shipping discounts

Poshmark has also added a shipping discount option, which can be an incentive for a buyer that's on the fence. Underneath the listing price, you can choose from three discount levels, including free shipping. Keep in mind, shipping discounts will be deducted from your proceeds and are only available for items that cost more than the current shipping rate.

For items that are listed at or above $500, Poshmark will automatically apply free shipping to your item without deducting it from your proceeds. Items that have free or discounted shipping will have a truck icon with a free or discounted shipping caption.

Figure 3.10 Example of listings with free shipping.

Although adding these details sounds like a lot, the listing process shouldn't take you long. When I started, I averaged approximately five minutes per listing. Today, it takes me about two (not including set-up). Once you get into a rhythm, you'll find that you can list items quickly and efficiently so you can allocate more time to selling and engaging.

Ok, let the sales rain in! (Not quite)

When we started, it took us about thirty minutes to set up a live store and list five-to-six items for sale. Upon first impression, this seemed to be the ideal solution we were missing out on during the year and a half we struggled with other platforms (I later found out that Poshmark has been around for several years – slap forehead).

We started getting followers to our store within the first hour. Over the next several weeks, once a week, I worked with my dad to list more items.

Then, crickets.

In the next chapter, I'll talk about a common mistake new sellers make on Poshmark; one that I became an "expert" on.

◑ BEST PRACTICE TIPS:
- o Snap photos of the front, back of the garment, close-ups of the top half and bottom, label (if applicable) and a size chart for multiple listings.
- o Use an app like Canva if you want to create grids so you can combine photos into one square.
- o Be upfront about any flaws, blemishes, or damage, especially with used clothing. Use photos to showcase. Transparency is key to a positive experience all around.
- o Poshmark recently added size charts to listing categories, which are linked next to sizes on a listing. However, it's not a bad idea to include a photo of a size chart, especially of a specific brand since sizes can vary across manufacturers. You can often find these online.
- o Be as specific as possible when answering questions on condition and sizing as this can lead to sales.
- o Avoid emojis in your title. Poshmark is part search engine, so listings are search engine optimized (SEO) based on words. I do have one emoji exception for inventory management, which I'll cover in a later chapter.
- o Add style tags to your listing to enhance its searchability.
- o The "Brand" menu field can only be changed three times so set it correctly the first time and leave it.

- **EXERCISE:** Find a space within your home or storefront to create listings. You don't need a professional studio. A nice corner of your home will do fine. Use that space to create consistent looking photos. Practice taking photos of multiple angles. Use a mannequin or ask a friend to be your model. Experiment and adjust lighting conditions as needed. You don't need fancy equipment. Often, a lamp or open window with daylight exposure will do just fine. If you build up your business and decide to invest more time, energy, and money, you can always upgrade your lighting and staging equipment later.

4 STORIES AND VIDEO

In the last chapter, we covered listing basics with a heavy emphasis on photos, which is Poshmark's primary visual marketing tool and similarly for all major ecommerce platforms, including Amazon, eBay, and Shopify. According to Poshmark, video has been one of the most requested features for the platform. When I first started writing this book, it was not an option. However, in 2020 and 2021, Poshmark gave sellers this coveted upgrade. I could not publish this book without a deep dive into this feature, which is why it's getting its own chapter.

Not surprisingly, more and more consumers are buying online and that includes what they wear. It always amazes me when we sell a wedding gown or high-end coat to someone who has never had a chance to try it on. What is surprising is that more sellers aren't using video now that it's been out for a while. I expected a flood of videos on new listings but currently, the majority of sellers aren't using it. However, I firmly believe that this will change and if you're starting out as a seller then grab the proverbial bull by the horns and stand out by putting video into all of your listings.

Poshmark first rolled out video with stories. Similar to Instagram, sellers can upload a photo or short video (up to 15 seconds) by clicking on the plus-sign next to their avatars within their closet. This immediately opens the camera with options to record videos on the spot or to upload photos or pre-recorded videos. Let's cover this feature first.

Stories are temporary, running for 24 hours. They're meant for engagement and marketing. You can use stories to let visitors know a little more about you, to highlight new or active listings, or even promote and shout out other Poshmark users. Poshmark stories allow you to add optional tags, including to specific Poshmark users, brands, and listings from your closet. You can also add text. It's very user friendly and takes a matter of minutes, if not seconds to create a story. Figure 4.1 demonstrates this feature using a photo. Note: you don't have to tag yourself as the story will automatically add a link to your closet. I've added a self-tag simply to demonstrate it as a feature.

To create a story:

1. Click the + on your avatar.
2. Select a photo or video to upload from your phone. You can also choose a listing.
3. The menu bar at the top allows you to tag a featured brand, one listing from your closet, and add text.
4. Hit the paper airplane icon and the story will be featured on your Poshmark store for 24 hours.

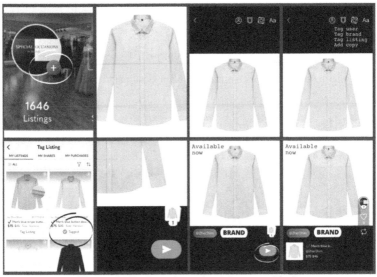

Figure 4.1 Poshmark stories (photo or video).

In 2021, after rolling out stories, Poshmark bridged the gap and added video capability to listings themselves. Now, sellers can post a short video of an item as part of a listing, also limited to 15 seconds or less. Again, I'm surprised that more sellers aren't using video because it makes a huge difference, especially if you're selling a high-end item that commands a premium price. Video simply shows greater depth and dimension that you just can't replicate with photos no matter how good they are. Now, you can use videos to highlight new listings and answer questions about garment details such as texture, form, and more.

I do have a theory as to why more sellers aren't using video. Fear. Video seems more complicated and time consuming than snapping photos. But how hard is it really to use video? It may sound intimidating when you're already busy enough trying to get the best photos and come up with snappy copy for your listing. After experimenting with a few different ways, I came up with a method that takes about three-to-five minutes.

First, I recommend don't film your video directly from the app. Of the videos I've seen on listings, many are simply shaky clips of the item on a hanger with poor lighting and a lot of background noise. Still, I believe that's better than not using video at all. However, I want you to stand out from day one. I'm going to break down how we create professional looking videos quickly and efficiently from a smartphone.

Second, use the same tips I shared in the last chapter for photos. Use a model or mannequin for your garments and a designated studio area with decent lighting.

Figure 4.2 Adding video to a listing.

I'll start with the really quick method (less than one minute):

1. Film your video separately on your phone rather than natively on the app.

2. Use portrait (tall mode) since it fits best with Poshmark's video feature.

3. Film the garment and walk around it to give a 360-degree view (similar to a "steady cam").

    a. Don't film in super high definition (HD) since that will make the file bigger and take much longer to upload. As long as you shoot in decent quality and good lighting, you're good to go.

    b. Start at the top-front, walk around the garment, capturing the side and back, until you circle back to where you started.

    c. If you can't do a complete walk-around, film two or three separate videos showcasing different angles.

    d. Keep your video short: no more than 15 seconds. Shorter is fine too (a complete walk around a mannequin or model should take anywhere from 12 – 14 seconds max).

4. The video will be stored in your album. Take a second to edit it by removing the background noise (squeaking shoes, talking, barking dogs, traffic, etc.). Most phones have this as a one-touch option.

5. Create the listing as you normally would, as covered in chapter three. When you get to the photos upload the video from your album. You can also add videos to listings you've already created.

If you follow these steps, you'll already stand out from most sellers with professional looking videos that add at most a minute or two to the listing creation process. Now, if you can spare another two-to-four minutes, I'll share what we do to really make these pop:

1. Follow the steps to create the video above.

2. Open a movie editor app such as iMovie (native on most iPhones) or equivalent if you have an Android.

    a. Pop in the clip(s).

    b. You may have to pinch to zoom out to ensure the aspect ratio is preserved (in other words the full portrait view).

    c. Add royalty-free music or sound effects (iMovie has a library).

    d. Record voiceover.

    e. Export the video to your album.

3. Once you've exported your movie, you may notice the video has a different aspect ratio depending on the editor app. In particular, portrait videos are surrounded by black bars on both sides making it widescreen.

   a. Edit the video within your album (most phones have this natively).

   b. Crop out the black bars.

   c. This will return it back to portrait (tall mode).

4. Upload the video to your Poshmark listing (this may take a minute or two depending on the length).

Reading this chapter will take you longer than creating a video for your listings or stories. Put in that extra effort and you will stand out in a great way, which will lead to more sales.

- **BEST PRACTICE TIP:** As a bonus, any videos you incorporate into your listings will automatically appear in your stories with tags back to the listing itself. I recommend keep your favorite or all of your videos on your phone. You can reuse and recycle these in your stories any time you want to highlight listings, making it evergreen marketing content.

- **EXERCISE:** Practice creating a listing video. Try getting it all in one shot, within 15 seconds, doing a 360 walk around your garment. Experiment with lighting, positioning, and your method.

- **BONUS EXERCISE:** Spruce up your video with music and / or voiceover. Come up with your own marketing style. Voiceover can be anything from explaining conditions, sizing, and colors to painting a picture of what occasion a particular listing might be great for.

5 THE ART OF PRICING LISTINGS

In chapter three, we looked at all the elements that go into a listing, including price. Now, let's dive into the art and science of pricing your listings on Poshmark. Because many of you may be selling on Poshmark as a side hustle; listing items you own but don't want or need anymore, I'll start with used items.

First, consider the condition of the item, starting with new (loosely defined as items you own but have never worn), then used items.

New items

If the item is "new with tags," meaning you bought it off the rack at a store or online and have never worn it, it's reasonable to list it for the price you paid for it or at a small discount. As an example, you bought a shirt for $40 that you never wore, and it still has the tags on it. You could list it for $40 or for a small discount, say $35 or $38, based on its condition. If you bought it on sale or at a special discount, you could even list it for the normal retail price to maximize your profit. This is known as "retail arbitrage." To illustrate further, say you purchased the same shirt, which normally retails for $40, at a Black Friday sale for $29.95. Assuming it's new with tags, you could list it for higher, say $37. This would be less than the full retail price but above what you paid for it.

Used items

With used items, you'll need to apply a different mindset for pricing. If you have used items you want to sell, the two most important factors are condition and age.

Condition: "Used" doesn't mean crappy

Regardless of how old the item is or how used, make sure it's clean and presentable. "Used" does not mean you can sell your 20-year-old sneakers that are falling apart at the seams. Make your listings attractive: polish those shoes, remove stains or scuff marks from jeans and dresses, and do the basics such as dry cleaning, ironing, and making minor repairs (e.g., fix hanging threads or loose buttons).

Age: Apply the "salvage value" mindset to older, used items

With older items, get into the mindset of "salvage value." This is a phrase I learned years ago in a business accounting course. It's commonly applied to office or farm equipment and refers to proceeds you make from a sale on an item after it's exhausted its shelf life. I won't get into the nitty-gritty of the accounting concept, which involves tax deductions and amortization. For our purposes, imagine you have an old computer. It's outdated, slow, and can't run the latest operating system, but it still works. You can't sell it for the original price or even close to that but if it's working, there's some value in it. Simply put, if you sell that computer for any amount, that money represents the computer's "salvage value."

Unlike new items you've only had for a few weeks or months, your old items have long lived out their shelf life. If you're no longer wearing them, they're not doing anything other than taking up valuable real estate in your closet and drawers. The goal with these items is to liquidate them and turn them into cash. Consider pricing them low so they're attractive to a buyer. Remember, be upfront about the condition in the description. If you're not sure what to use as a list price, look for similar listings in a similar condition, either on Poshmark or elsewhere to get an idea.

Even if you don't make much money on the sale, that's money you now have in exchange for an item that you aren't using anymore. The more you're able to get rid of, the more space you'll free up while adding cash to your coffers. While a few bucks may not seem like a lot for an old pair of shoes or a shirt, it adds up as you sell more items.

Wholesale

If you're in the clothing business or you've upped your Poshmark game by buying wholesale, pricing is about profit margin. What is wholesale? Essentially, you're buying items in bulk from a supplier rather than individually at a store. A supplier is usually a third party that gets its clothes directly from a manufacturer and sells them exclusively business-to-business (B2B) to retail stores. Today, wholesale is no longer just limited to businesses like my dad's. Poshmark has a program that allows individual sellers to buy from select wholesalers. Moreover, platforms like Amazon, Shein, Alibaba, and AliExpress provide access to tons of suppliers both in the US and overseas. Buying wholesale allows you to get a lot of an item while paying less per unit. The business then adds a markup, usually 30-40% over cost. While that sounds high, keep in mind, the sale price is the fair market value (i.e., what a buyer is willing to pay for it) and the retail business must buy a large quantity to pay a lower per unit cost. The markup represents the profit, which is a business's lifeblood. This is what pays the bills, keeps the lights on, and pays the employees. Think of it as the equivalent of buying bulk at Costco.

Don't sacrifice profitability for sales

Finally, you may be wondering if it is worth it to price new or barely used items at an unusually low price to gain traction and generate reviews. This is known as "loss leading," in which you sacrifice profitability, even to the point of taking a loss, to generate sales momentum. Opinions vary on this, but I don't think this is necessary, and may be detrimental to your long-term success as it can create an expectancy for extremely low prices. I'll talk more about negotiating principles in a later chapter. But, if you're selling an item that's worth a lot of money, you should try to get as close to its fair market value as possible.

EXERCISE: As you list your items, consider the condition, age, and profit margin or salvage value. If you're new to this, write it out. This will eventually become second nature.

Item	
• Original price	
• Age and Condition	
• Profit margin or salvage value	

We will build off this in chapter eight, when we look at negotiating sales.

6 POSHMARK SAFETY 101 ("AVOID STRANGER DANGER")

Since we're at the point, in which you're setting up your store and creating your first Poshmark listings, now is a good time to talk about ecommerce safety.

When you post your first item, the listing will have buttons to purchase it at the listed price or tender an offer. In addition, the listing will resemble a social media post; allowing people to interact with it by liking, sharing, or asking questions. We'll cover these more in depth later but for now, the comment section is a great way for potential buyers to engage with you and vice versa. Most message posts will be earnest questions, which you can reply to directly. However, there is one type of message, which you should never respond to.

When we started with our first listings in May 2018, we sometimes got posts asking us to contact a phone number or email address, asking if an item was still available or an outright offer to pay full price or more. Often, we would see the same message copied and pasted several times for multiple listings.

Being a natural skeptic, I immediately smelled something fishy. Let me save you the suspense. These are not buyers but spammers and scammers trying to lure you outside of Poshmark to trick you out of your money and / or your listing. If you did your homework earlier and searched for articles on Poshmark, you may have come across horror stories of Poshmark sellers scammed out of their money and their items through elaborate schemes involving invitations to communicate outside of the app by phone or email, along with PayPal accounts or money wires. Often, you'll see the same messages copy and pasted from different garbage accounts (see photo below) that have no photo, have recently been set up, and use gibberish for their Poshmark handles. Fortunately, fake accounts are easy to spot. However, some of the more sophisticated spammers will put a little more effort to create real sounding Poshmark names and even add profile pics. Others will post to advertise other apps, platforms, or something else entirely.

If you happen to see messages like that, your inner red flag should go up. Don't respond, simply hit the flag button underneath the message and the moderators will remove it right away.

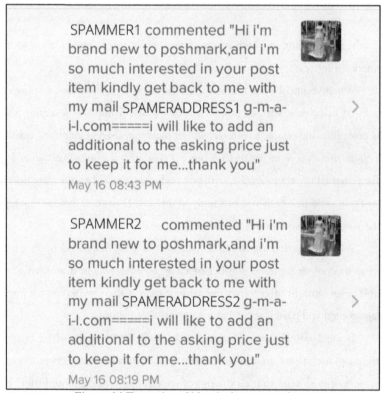

Figure 6.1 Examples of identical spam postings.

If you continue getting spammed by the same account or multiple ones copying and pasting the same message, click on their profile to block and report them.

Legit buyers will **never** have a reason to buy from you outside of Poshmark. For a buyer, it doesn't cost them anything extra to buy within the app and the ecosystem is designed to protect both buyer and seller. If you're a seller, you don't want the headaches of dealing with scams so stay within the app. You pay the commission fees to participate within a safe ecosystem. Don't fall prey to these messages. As we've covered, Poshmark's fees are deducted from your sales but it's far safer to buy and sell within the ecosystem than risk venturing outside of it.

Unfortunately, spam or scam postings are a fact of virtual life. While Poshmark has done a better job of cracking down hard on spammers, often catching and removing these posts right away, spam messages still appear from time to time. There have been occasions when we would post three or four listings and would immediately see replies using a copy and paste message from fake Poshmark accounts.

For those of you who are new, know that you will get hit with these from time to time. We'll dive into how transactions work shortly but just remember the lesson you learned as a kid about "stranger danger" and avoid contacting buyers outside of the app. There's no reason for you to do so and it's not worth the risk.

However, if you're running a Poshmark store as part of a retail business, there are times when you may have legitimate buyers earnestly asking about a listing and whether they can visit your physical location. Since it's obvious from our photos that we are a retail shop and not an individual seller, we sometimes get inquiries about our store. We've even had customers visit and purchase directly from us. I will cover this more in depth in a later chapter. However, I only recommend engaging in in-person visits and interactions if you have a physical retail space. For you individual and solo sellers, stay within the app!

- **EXERCISE:** Pop Quiz. If someone posts a message asking you to contact them directly by email or phone to buy the item you've listed, you:
    A. Report it as SPAM
    B. Report is as SPAM
    C. Report is as SPAM
    D. Report is as SPAM

7 ADMITTING THE MISTAKE I MADE (SO YOU WON'T REPEAT IT)

In chapter two, I talked about the advantages of setting up a store on Poshmark, highlighting it as a true "out of the box" platform to sell clothes. While the setup was easy and listing items was a matter of snapping a few photos, writing simple copy, and using pull-down menus, sales didn't just rain in.

We started in May 2018 and over subsequent weeks, I worked with my dad to create new listings every Wednesday. As we did, people started following us, liking items, and leaving comments. However, we didn't generate any sales. In fact, we didn't hit our first sale until August of that year.

Figure 7.1 Our first sale on Poshmark.

Why did it take us so long to generate a sale?

I made a huge mistake.

I treated Poshmark like a passive sales platform: a "list it and leave it" place to list products, slap a price, and nothing more. I completely missed the point of the platform and a key component to generating momentum and sales.

Poshmark isn't just a "garage sale" table, in which you put out your wares. It's an entire community that shares attributes with today's most prolific social media platforms. Unlike Amazon or Shopify, which you might combine with external social media like Facebook, Twitter, and Instagram to promote your listings, Poshmark has many of the same features baked right in.

I didn't engage in this community as much as I could or should have. When someone liked our products or followed our store, I didn't follow back. When someone shared our listings, I didn't share back. In other words, I sat back and waited for sales to happen.

They didn't. Imagine trying several platforms over the course of a year, none of them are a good fit, and all include their share of end-user pain points. Then, you stumble onto a platform that works out of the box, is user-friendly, mobile, and yet, you're still not generating sales. By summer 2018, I was ready to give up. I started doubting myself and regretting ever suggesting online sales. It felt like a pipe dream.

Then, I took another look. Clearly, we had the listing process down. We had quality clothes and decent photos with good lighting and descriptive text. That wasn't the issue. There had to be something else and once I played around with the platform and read some more articles and blogs on Poshmark, it hit me.

Poshmark isn't simply a sales platform but a community with its own ecosystem. Once I realized this, I changed my approach.

- I followed people on Poshmark, both sellers and buyers.
- I shared other people's listings when they shared ours.
- I proactively shared other people's listings even when they didn't share ours.
- And the biggest game changer, I started attending Poshmark parties: designated hours, in which Poshers engage and share items that fit within a specific category or theme. We'll cover this more in a later chapter.

Sounds a little counterintuitive, right? Sharing someone else's listings and following other Poshmark sellers isn't a traditional business tactic. It's almost as if I was encouraging my followers to shop elsewhere. That might be true if I was advertising a local business down the street, and we were competing for the same customers in the neighborhood. But Poshmark isn't local. It has millions of users across the country (now globe), generating millions of sales. Sharing someone else's dress or coat wasn't going to take away from my dad's business. Rather, a communal sharing approach: I share your item, you share mine, gets both of our items in front of a larger market. The more you share, the more proactive you are, the more other sellers and buyers will follow you and see what you have to offer. If you're just getting started, here's a great hack to identify potential customers and build up a following. I learned this one from Ashley Waters Gordon, a fellow Posher who's been on the platform for several years. If you sell specialty items, for example medical scrubs, search Poshmark usernames using topical key words such as "medical" or "medstudent." Follow those people. Often, Poshmark buyers will add theme words or phrases that identify the kind of goods they're looking for. In our case, since we primarily sell wedding, prom, and special occasion wear, we would follow users that have words like "bride," "wedding" or "prom" in them. Make those connections, introduce yourself if they're new by posting a welcome message, and you may end up with a customer. Poshmark's algorithm will also do a lot of the heavy lifting for you. Once you start closing sales, and if you become a Poshmark Ambassador (which I'll cover later), the platform will start leading new users to your store. By taking a proactive approach, you're setting yourself up for success.

Once I became more proactive, our listings garnered more followers, more likes, and more shares. I could see this on a real time basis as my phone lit up with more alert notifications than when I was simply passive. I received so many notifications that I had to silence the ones for sharing, likes, and follows. Eventually, we completed our first sale in August: a pair of designer blue jeans. It wasn't a huge sale, but it was a wonderful breakthrough that validated our efforts in pursuing an online sales channel.

While Poshmark has proven to be a wonderful solution for individuals who want to clean out their closets, it helped transform my dad's brick and mortar clothing business; helping keep it afloat during the pandemic in 2020 and 2021. Currently, my dad's business is not the average Poshmark seller demographic, but I firmly believe that more retail sellers will be using it and similar platforms as a go-to ecommerce solution. Buying clothes online is here to stay. We're noticing the stickiness of certain shopper habits as we exit the pandemic. As I'm writing this chapter, we're recovering our in-person traffic while our Poshmark sales continue to grow. Moreover, Poshmark adds a bargaining element similar to eBay but without the word "auction." Buyers and sellers can negotiate with price offers, comments, and timed sales. All of these features are baked in, making it an organic part of the platform.

That said, most people selling on Poshmark are just like you: individuals like Ashley who are in grad school or working a fulltime job or running other businesses and are spending their spare hours building a business or side hustle online.

If one of your goals this year is to start a small side business, spend some time on your branding (chapter two) so you can make the best first impression.

⟡ **EXERCISE:** If you completed the last exercise, your account should be set up. If not, now would be a good time to do that since we'll be building up your virtual shop throughout the rest of this book.

For a review of listing basics, go back to chapter three.

Once you have created your first listings, start engaging within the Poshmark community.

- o **Share** your items and listings on a regular basis. Don't just let them sit there. Try to do this at least once a day, if not a couple times a week.
- o **Follow** people who engage with you and your store with likes, shares, and comments.
- o **Reciprocate:** if someone shares your item, share one or more of theirs.
- o **Communicate:** if someone posts a question, it means they're interested. Respond in a timely manner.
- o **Attend Poshmark Parties:** these are great opportunities to showcase your listings and connect with potential buyers. We'll cover parties in greater detail in a separate chapter.

PART II

8 A DEEP DIVE INTO SALES AND TRANSACTIONS

Thus far, we've talked about best practices for creating listings, pricing, and Poshmark safety. Now, let's turn our attention to transactions and how they work on the platform.

Understanding how sales work

Once you've listed an item for sale, there are two selling scenarios you'll come across:

Figure 8.1 Offer and Buy Now.

Scenario 1: "Buy now"

The buyer wants to buy your item outright at the listed price. There is no negotiating involved. It's vital that you have the item in stock so if you're selling both off and online as in the case of a retail business, keep your inventory current.

Scenario 2: "Offer"

When you receive an offer, a prospective buyer tenders a price that is below what you've listed the item for. Once you receive an offer, you have 24 hours to decide what you want to do. You have three options:

1. **Accept:** you agree to the offer, which turns the transaction into a closed sale.

2. **Decline:** you decline the offer outright, which allows the buyer to tender a new offer or move on.

3. **Counter:** you submit a price that's above the original offer for the buyer to consider within a 24-hour window, in which they may accept, counter, or decline.

    a. **Match Buyer's Last Offer:** Poshmark recently added what I call a "boomerang" option. You can replace your counteroffer with a new one that will match the buyer's last offer.

Offers occur within a private window between you and the buyer. Poshmark is a true marketplace, in which buyer and seller can negotiate price. We'll cover negotiations in a separate chapter.

Once a sale goes through within either scenario, you will receive a notification within the app and by email that the item has been sold along with a shipping label. The listing will be marked with a "sold" stamp and will no longer be available for anyone else to buy it.

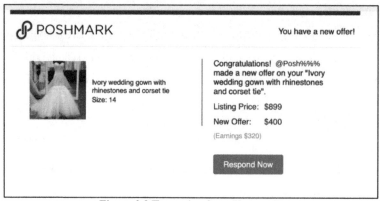

Figure 8.2 Example of an offer email.

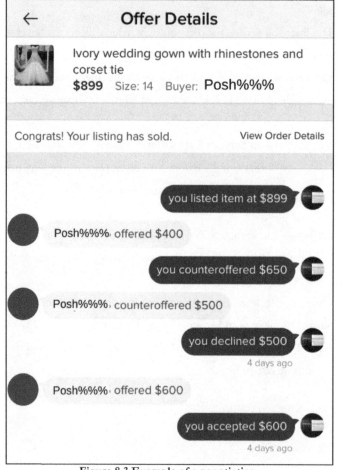

Figure 8.3 Example of a negotiation.

Preparing a sold item for shipping

Next, prepare and ship the item to your customer. Poshmark recommends you ship orders within two to three days. If you do not ship within seven days, the buyer can cancel and get a full refund. Sales that are not shipped after 21 days are automatically cancelled. My advice is, once a sale closes, ship it right away: same or next day.

Step 1: Identify and inspect the item

The first thing you should do is make sure you have the correct item. This is crucial, especially if you've listed several items that resemble one another. This is where cross-checking size, color, and SKU really come in handy. The last thing you want to do is ship out the wrong item or size. Once you identify the item, inspect it to make sure it matches the description exactly. If there are blemishes, scuff marks, or damage, make sure it is noted in the description. As you can't change the description for a sold item (for obvious reasons), if for some reason you notice the item has some defect that isn't listed, communicate this to the buyer right away. Let them know and offer to cancel the sale if they do not wish to proceed with the purchase. If the buyer receives the merchandise with a defect that was not previously disclosed, they will have the right to file a complaint and apply for a refund and return. If the buyer wishes to see the damage first, create a dummy listing with photos showcasing the damage or defect and tag the buyer.

Step 2: Pack the item

When it comes to packing items, do so with care. This is especially important if it's a delicate item such as a silk dress with sequins or a bag with pearls. How you pack your item is as much a reflection of you and your customer service as the item itself. For small items, zip lock bags are great for extra security before placing into a box. For larger items, wrap them in plastic or tissue paper. Don't just throw them into a box.

For articles such as dresses and coats, fold them neatly and if you can, cover them with plastic or pack them with the original garment bag if it came with one and you still have it. When it comes to hangers, I generally don't include them since the hooks may potentially damage the item in transit. If I include a hanger, such as a name brand one that goes with a designer coat, I make sure to wrap the hook in plastic or tape it up so the end can't tear into the fabric.

Next, place the wrapped item into a box that matches the size of the item. You can use leftover boxes you have in stock or in your closet. If you reuse a box, make sure to remove or mark out any old mailing labels and barcodes.

You can also use USPS priority shipping boxes. You can pick these up for free at any post office or order them from their website at https://store.usps.com/store/home. USPS boxes come in a variety of sizes, including small ones for items such as jewelry to medium to larger ones that are ideal for suits, coats, and dresses. You can even get specific boxes for shoes. However, you cannot use boxes that are labelled "express."

Before we move on, there is one real world wrinkle I want to share. Although Poshmark's guidelines say you can use priority <u>flat rate</u> boxes, I've had inconsistent experiences at the post office when shipping items with these. At times, I've experienced no issue and other times, I've been told I can't use a priority flat rate box. I've contacted Poshmark about this and although they confirmed that any non-express box, including flat rate ones, can be used for Poshmark shipping, for safety, I recommend sticking with non-flat rate priority boxes.

Step 3: Print out and affix the shipping label

As mentioned, once you sell an item, you'll automatically get an email with a sales notification and a PDF of the shipping label. Poshmark customers typically purchase shipping along with the item. We'll cover how to offer a shipping discount in a future chapter. You can use any standard printer to print these out. As you grow your Poshmark business, you may want to invest in a thermal label printer for shipping labels. Be sure to get one that can handle 4" × 6" labels. If for some reason you do not get the email label, check your junk mail folder. If it's not there, go into the app, click on "My Sales," then click on the item you sold and "Need New Shipping Label" to resend it.

Once you receive your label, double check to make sure it's the correct one. I repeat, double check the label. As you generate more sales, you'll receive more emails, more sales notifications, and labels. This is a good thing, but it also means you must be diligent about making sure the items and labels are correct. Ensure the confirmation email matches the item you are packing and the Poshmark username of the buyer, which is printed on the label. Once you receive the label and confirm it is correct, print it out, and tape it to the box.

As mentioned, shipping is covered by a standard flat rate label. Typically, your buyer will purchase shipping in addition to the item itself (plus applicable sales tax, which Poshmark automatically assesses by state). You can offer to include shipping to incentivize your buyer, which I'll cover in a later chapter. The standard shipping label is a flat rate that covers up to five pounds.

For items that are heavier than five pounds such as large dresses or bundles of two or more items, Poshmark gives you the option to purchase additional shipping; located in a menu within "My Sales." Currently, additional shipping is charged to the seller and deducted out of proceeds. You can also purchase additional shipping on top of the five-pound label at your post office. Fortunately, most clothes, even coats and large dresses are fine with the standard shipping rate.

Figure 8.4 Example of Poshmark mail label and package.

Step 4: Ship out the package

Once you have packed your item and labeled it, it's time to ship it out to your buyer. Currently, all Poshmark items are shipped by USPS using two to three-day priority mail. If you have a USPS location nearby, you can go there during normal business hours to drop off the package. If the line isn't long, you can get the packaged scanned and get a receipt noting the date and time, along with the tracking number from the label. I generally do this when I have time or when shipping an expensive item. Otherwise, if the line is long or you don't have time to wait, most post offices have a space where you can leave pre-labelled packages. Do not drop packages into a blue mailbox since most priority mail shipping boxes aren't designed to fit.

Some locations have after-hours access, in which you can drop off packages into a tumbler. If your post office has this, it's a great way to get your packages out after standard work hours if you're doing this as a side hustle. It's also great for getting packages out on Sundays and holidays when the post office is closed.

Finally, you can schedule an in-person pickup of your packages. In the email with your shipping label, you will see a link to schedule a free USPS package pickup. If you have a steady stream of orders, you may want to speak to your local post office or mail person to see if they can make picking up Poshmark packages a regular part of their daily mail service to you. Not all are able to do this so ask before leaving a package out. Otherwise use the aforementioned package pickup link as needed. Make sure you have a way for them to pick up packages securely or hand it to them personally (example if you're working from home) rather than leaving them somewhere where they can be stolen.

Figure 8.5 USPS self-service kiosk and package tumbler.

Step 5: Confirm the shipment

Once the package is out for delivery, go into "My Sales" and confirm that you've shipped out the package. Check off the following three boxes:

- Print postage label and pack item.
- Drop off item at post office.
- Confirm that the package has been shipped out.

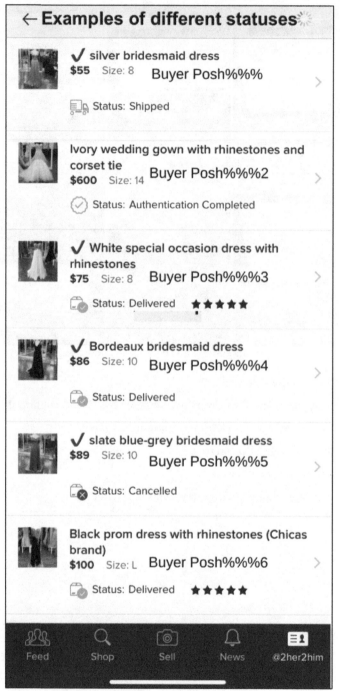

Figure 8.6 Poshmark order status list.

After you check the three tasks and submit it, the status will change from "Sold" to "Shipped." Once USPS updates its system, the status will change from "Shipped" to "Tracking." If the status doesn't change right away, don't panic. It can take anywhere from one hour to a full day for USPS tracking to activate, even if you get the package scanned right away.

Once you've shipped your item, let the buyer know by tagging them in a comment underneath the sold item or within a bundle chat.

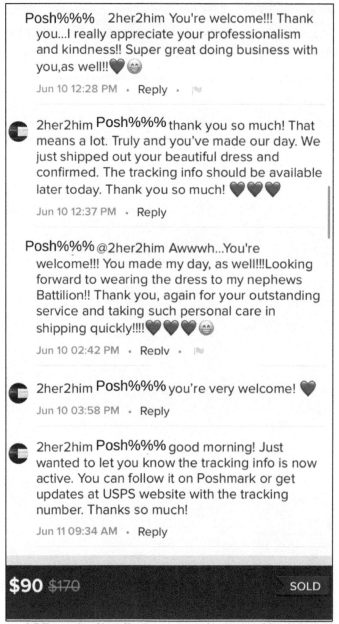

Figure 8.7 Example of bundle chat communicating tracking information.

Additional note about shipping

During 2020-21, USPS experienced unprecedented delays due to massively increased shipping loads. As I'm writing this, shipments have returned to their usual two–to-three day period but know that occasionally packages may take longer. Even before the pandemic, we would have the one-off package that would be in transit for a week or longer. Package tracking and keeping your customer informed are part of making a Poshmark shopping experience a positive one.

If a shipment is taking an unusually long time to get to a customer, notify them. Thank them for their patience and remind them that they can check the progress of the shipment using the tracking number but keep an eye on it. If a shipment is taking longer than ten days to deliver, notify Poshmark.

In the event that a shipment is lost by the post office, Poshmark will reimburse both buyer and seller. We've had this happen twice. This is another reason it's a good idea to stay within the app for transactions.

Order cancellations

Now that we've covered standard shipping procedures, let's cover cancellations. If a buyer purchases an item at full price ("buy it now"), they can cancel it within the first three hours. If that happens, you'll get a notification asking you not to send the item. Therefore, if you get a "buy it now" purchase, you can start prepping and packing the item but wait until the grace period passes before shipping it. You won't be able to confirm it until then.

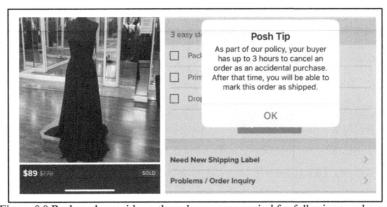

Figure 8.8 Poshmark provides a three-hour grace period for full price purchases.

After the grace period expires, the item is considered sold and you can ship it. Alternatively, if the buyer purchases an item from a 24-hour sale (we'll cover timed discounts later) or from a negotiated price that is lower than the list price, the sale is considered final.

That said, you may run into a situation, in which the sale is past the cancellation period or final by negotiated offer and the buyer communicates that they want to cancel. In that case, only you as the seller can authorize a cancellation. You can click on the order and cancel it. Although the sale is considered "final," I generally cancel orders if a buyer does not wish to go through with it so long as I haven't already shipped and confirmed the sale. Let me share two real world situations, in which we did so and why.

Scenario 1: "the ghost"

Once, we had a customer place an order and we prepared to ship it out the next day. However, the customer then asked if we could cancel the order because the shipping address was incorrect. We cancelled the order and let her know; allowing her the opportunity to update her address and repurchase it. She never ended up buying it again. I suspect she changed her mind and didn't want the item after all.

Scenario 2: "wrong fit"

Another time, a customer purchased a dress from a "Black Friday" sale we ran with a timed discount. After making the purchase, she let us know that she liked the dress she ordered but that it was way too big for her. In that situation, we could have shipped the dress since she bought it from a sale and had no right or option to cancel. However, we cancelled it for her.

You may be wondering why we did this in both scenarios even though both sales were final. In both cases, the customer would not have been happy with their purchase. In the first, we weren't going to risk sending it to the wrong address. The fact that she didn't re-purchase it just means she wasn't interested. In the second, we didn't want to sell an item that obviously wouldn't be a good fit for the customer. In these situations, you're better off cancelling the sale. You'll minimize the risk of negative reviews, complaints, and unhappy customers.

Post-sales

Barring the above-scenarios and assuming you've smoothly closed the sale, shipped, and confirmed, the item(s) will take anywhere from two to three days (or slightly longer depending on the current state of USPS) to deliver. As noted, a best practice I recommend is to let the customer know you've shipped and confirmed. You can also keep them posted along the way. I often do this for expensive or high-end items such as wedding gowns or when the post office is experiencing unusual delays. Keeping a customer informed demonstrates extra care and can mean the difference between a four-star and five-star rating.

Once the buyer receives the item, the status will change from "Tracking" to "Delivered." The customer has three days to inspect the item, in which time, they can do one of three things.

Scenario 1: Accept the item

This means, the buyer has accepted the purchase, which will close the transaction and disburse the proceeds into your Poshmark account.

Scenario 2: Wait the three-day period

Sometimes, a buyer will not accept right away. Once the three-day waiting period expires, the transaction will close on the fourth day and the money will be disbursed into your account. Don't panic if this happens. There are many reasons why a buyer may not accept right away. Moreover, this is not necessarily a sign of anything wrong. Don't push the buyer to accept. Simply allow them the time and wait it out. Most of the time, the sale will close smoothly, and the proceeds will release on the fourth day.

Scenario 3: Open a case

If there's a problem or issue, the customer can report it to Poshmark. This will open a case, in which Poshmark will act as a mediator to hear both sides and decide whether to allow for a return and refund, or to close the sale as final. We'll cover this in more detail in a later chapter.

Figure 8.9 Example of a flaw disclosure in a Poshmark listing.

Proceeds

Assuming the transaction closes by immediate acceptance or after the three-day inspection period tolls, the status will change from "Delivered" to "Order Closed" and the proceeds (net Poshmark's commission) will be transferred into your Poshmark account. From there, you can hold it in your account to use as payment for a purchase if you shop on Poshmark, or you can transfer the proceeds via direct bank deposit or check.

Procedures for selling items over $500

I've alluded to some best practices when selling high-end items such as wedding gowns. Poshmark also has slightly different procedures for expensive listings such as jewelry or designer name-brand items: specifically, ones that are listed at $500 or more. These are classified as premium or "luxury" items. Once you close a sale on an item that falls into that range, Poshmark sends you a label that ships the item to an inspection facility where it's inspected before being sent to the customer. Upon arrival, Poshmark authenticates it to make sure it's genuine, in good condition, and otherwise meets with the item description. This protects the buyer from potential fraud. Once approved, Poshmark sends it directly to the customer to close the sale. In this case, delivery to the customer takes longer than two to three days: up to a week or longer. I recommend notifying the customer that the item will be shipped to Poshmark for inspection and giving them a heads-up of the longer delivery time.

When selling high-end items, the same suggestions apply that we've been covering throughout this book. These include using good photos of multiple angles, adding video with robust descriptions, answering lots of questions, and taking photos of the item before you ship it out. In other words, don't treat your high-end items differently from anything else you sell. Rather, treat all your items as if they were high-end.

Standing out as a seller

To close this chapter, it's worth reiterating some of the best practices that will help you stand out as a seller. If there's one must, it's to communicate and confirm. Once a buyer has purchased your item, post a thank you message and tag them. Let them know that you've shipped and confirmed it. Some sellers go as far as to include personalized notes or small gifts with the item. That's up to you. But at the very minimum, tag them on posts to let them know you've shipped with care and to express your thanks.

Once someone purchases an item, send it out right away. One of the easiest and most effective ways you can stand out as a Poshmark seller is to send out your packages on the same or next day. Don't sit on orders. Poshmark will cancel transactions if too much time passes. If you want great reviews and repeat business, take each sale seriously and be prompt in sending out orders.

Finally, do not promise delivery dates. As you grow your business, buyers may ask if they can get an item by a certain date, especially if they need it right away. The most you can offer is to ship it out right away and say it generally takes two to three days via priority mail, not counting Sundays and federal holidays. During our first two years on Poshmark, deliveries were two-to-three days like clockwork. The 2020-21 pandemic upended everything with an exponential increase in shipping times. Online ordering is now a regular part of our lives when it comes to food, staples, gifts, and clothing. Shipments can and sometimes do take longer. You have no control over how or when the post office will deliver something so never promise a delivery date. Rather, provide information on how quickly you can ship it out and a general timeframe for deliveries. It's also a good practice to mention if the post office is experiencing unusual shipping delays and refer them to the tracking information.

In the next chapters, we'll dive deeper into other areas to help maximize sales, including Poshmark parties, item sharing, and negotiation strategies.

- ➋ **BEST PRACTICE TIPS:**
  - o Be upfront about the condition of your listings, especially used items. Over-communicate with pictures, video, and descriptions. Use a platform like Canva to create photos that highlight flaws or blemishes (see Figure 8.9 as an example).
  - o Take photos of the actual sold item from multiple angles, including close-ups of zippers, clasps, buttons, etc. Save the pictures into an album on your phone labelled "current orders." Keep these until the sale has finalized and the proceeds have been released.
  - o Cover up any open corners or open seams with packing tape to ensure the package is secure. Use clear packing tape to cover the address to make sure it doesn't get smudged out.
  - o USPS kiosks are available at many locations, which allow you to scan pre-printed labels (see Figure 8.5).
  - o After you ship the item, you can go to USPS.com, enter the tracking number from the label, and get text message or email updates. This is a good practice for first-time sellers.
  - o Notify your customer that you have packed, shipped, and confirmed their purchase.

- ➋ **EXERCISE ("Practice Gratitude"):** When you land your first sale, take a moment to savor the feeling and really understand what this means. Someone is trusting you to fulfill a need. For us, it was a pair of blue jeans. With each subsequent sale, remember the rush, the excitement, and appreciation you felt with your first sale. Pack and ship each item with care, knowing that your customer is excited to receive something that they will wear for a wedding, special occasion, job interview, holiday party, or first date.

9 THE ART OF NEGOTIATING ON POSHMARK

"You've got to know when to hold 'em, know when to fold 'em, know when to walk away." – Kenny Rogers (*The Gambler*)[4]

Now that we've covered the basics on listings and transactions, let's take a closer look at pricing, and negotiating offers. A few years ago, I was having coffee with a friend of mine (we'll call her "Lucy") who was working in marketing and meeting planning for a real estate company. Lucy was always fashionable, sporting the latest designer clothes and handbags, and when she learned that I was selling on Poshmark, she asked me about it. My dad and I had been on the platform for almost a year, and I shared our experiences up to that point, which inspired her to give it a whirl. She listed an expensive name brand purse, a Fendi or Louis Vuitton, that she had only used once or twice, meaning it was basically brand new. When she received an offer that was only half her listing price, she reluctantly accepted and immediately regretted it.

I call this "seller's remorse." I asked her why she sold it when she knew the offer was too low. Lucy's response was that she wasn't sure she'd ever get another one. You may have heard the phrase FOMO: "fear of missing out." For Poshmark sellers, I've come up with a slight variation: FOPO or "Fear of One Poshmark Offer."[5]

When you get your first offer, you'll feel an adrenaline rush as the alert hits your phone. There's a strong psychological pull that comes with it, no matter the amount. An offer is an indication that a person is willing and ready to buy your item. Respect that, embrace that, celebrate that. BUT don't accept it, if it's not within your target selling price range or what we'll refer to as the "Zone of Agreement" (ZOA).[6] More on this later.

Recall from chapter five, I briefly discussed that it's not in your best interest to take a "loss leader" position, in which you accept offers that are significantly below market value to generate sales and reviews. The reason is illustrated in the example above. You'll know in your gut that the sale doesn't reflect the item's value. If you make it a habit, it will make it that much harder to negotiate future sales since all sold items appear on your Poshmark closet along with the price at which it sold. As a result, savvy buyers can see what others paid for the same item. That's not to say that you can't negotiate different or even higher prices for the same item. Factors, including time of year (holidays vs. summer), scarcity and availability can justify higher (or lower as the case may be) prices. However, if you price your items too low that will send a signal to other buyers that make it harder to justify a fair market price for the item. What you don't want is for buyers to see you as the "discount" or "bargain basement" seller. The minor caveat is for old, used items that you're trying to clear from your closet, in which case, use the salvage value principle of turning your old items into cash.

Offers: say "no" when it's too low

When it comes to newer or premium items, including collectibles and name brand luxury items, don't accept the first offer that comes your way if it's too low. Since Poshmark is mostly geared towards reselling used items, most sellers discount anywhere between 20-40% off the original price paid or its retail value. Anything below that and you're being asked to give up additional value. In the case of an old item that you no longer care about, it might be worth taking such an offer. However, in the case items like Lucy's purse, taking anything substantially below the list price might lead to seller's regret and FOPO. While this sounds like common sense, if you're a first-time seller, you may feel a psychological pressure or "tug" to accept a lowball offer. It's a powerful feeling to have an offer come your way. You may feel that you'll never get a better one, or you may even doubt whether you've priced it correctly. Put those fears aside. If an offer is too low, decline it. Remember, Poshmark is a big place and if one person tenders an offer, chances are others will too. For my dad's business, we've had many occasions when we've declined offers and it's important to let go of that doubt. Often, declining an offer led us to get a better one or an outright sale at the list price from another buyer.

Pricing basics

Let's cover a methodology that has served us well and may be helpful to you if you're a first-time seller on Poshmark.

Fair market value

In pricing your items, look at the condition, age, and "satisfaction quotient," which we'll explore in greater detail below. If you're not sure what you paid for it originally, try looking it up online. If it's a newer item, it should be available for sale somewhere. Use the "fair market value" as a guidepost for setting the original price and a baseline to establish a discount list price. If it's an older item, set the original price close to what you paid for it. You may have to guestimate but don't stray too far. I've seen sellers list ridiculously high original prices for items that aren't anywhere in the same neighborhood as what they probably cost.

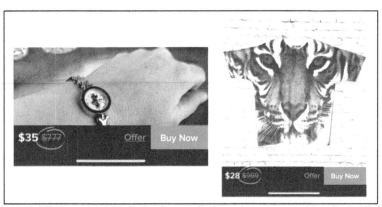

Figure 9.1 Examples of original prices on listings that are probably a little off the mark.

The "satisfaction" quotient

Once you've set a fair market price, consider your satisfaction quotient, which I think of as a sliding scale. Satisfaction can be defined as your happiness, your profit margin, your gut, your "mojo." There are two levels of satisfaction:

Level 1: Max satisfaction

This can be quantified as listing and selling an item without a discount. This would include what you paid for the item, what it's worth, or the fair market value. This number represents maximum satisfaction. It's the ideal world. If someone were to buy something at or even above what you paid for it (see chapter five's discussion of "retail arbitrage"), you would achieve max satisfaction. You would have no regrets and wear a big smile on your face after closing the deal.

Level 2: Optimal satisfaction

This is the next level and what your goal should be for most sales on Poshmark. In our experience, it's rare to hit max satisfaction. It happens but it's not the norm. On Poshmark, most items are discounted from the original price. For example, let's say the original price you paid for an item is $500 but you decide to sell it for $450 or $400. You are offering a discount and giving up a small slice of satisfaction to facilitate a sale. Perhaps it's used but in near-new condition as in the case of Lucy's purse. Or similar to my dad's situation, you bought it wholesale (see chapter five) and are still clearing a healthy profit margin by selling it at a discount from the normal retail markup. Optimal satisfaction is when a buyer buys your item outright at the discounted list price without any haggling or offers. There's no further loss of satisfaction other than what you've already given up in listing the item at a discounted price.

Below optimal satisfaction, you are entering into the wide realm of offers and negotiation that can be confusing and overwhelming. Here are some guideposts to help you navigate this.

Bounds and the zone of agreement (ZOA)

First, think of negotiating as a balance between the amount of satisfaction you're willing to give up and a price that a buyer is willing to pay for your item. If you agree to sell at any price below your list price, you are giving up a degree of satisfaction. You're compromising to sell the item and turn it into cash. As this gap increases, eventually the seller experiences regret for the transaction or "seller's remorse."

Next, it's helpful to have some bounds. Picture an upper bound, a lower bound, and an area in between.

Lower bound

Let's start with the lower bound first because this is what is most confusing for buyers and sellers. Think of the lower bound as a floor, an absolute minimum such that any price below that, it's not worth selling the item. It's not even worth trying to counter-offer because it's too far off the mark. Do NOT think of a lower bound as a "bottom line sale price." One of my biggest pet peeves is when a buyer asks, "what's the lowest price you'll accept?" My answer is usually the sale price on the listing. The sale price is the lowest price and reflects the level of satisfaction I'm willing to give up. If I'm open to negotiating the price or entertaining an offer, that simply means I may consider giving up more satisfaction. A lower bound should **never** be thought of as a price you will sell at if it's offered. If you get an offer that's right at or slightly above the lower bound, you may or may not decide to sell it at that price. A lot of factors go into making that decision, both financial and personal. It is simply a line underneath which you will decline any offers.

Upper bound

The upper bound is a price that's below your list price but close to it. The upper bound can be defined as the sale price itself but if you're open to negotiating, come up with a number in your head that's a little lower. As with the lower bound, you won't necessarily sell at that price though you're more likely to accept since it's closer to your list price. Remember, the bounds are simply guideposts.

71

The zone of agreement (ZOA)

The ZOA is an in-between area, in which an offer falls somewhere between the upper and lower bounds. Depending on the item and circumstances (e.g., your desire to sell it, how much space you will free up, how many of the items you have, etc.), the ZOA represents a price range in which you're willing to consider selling. If an offer falls in this zone, you may decide to sell, you may counter, or you may decline altogether. It's not meant to be a hard and fast area nor a "bottom line."

When you start listing and pricing your items, think of an imaginary upper and lower bound. You can write these down or keep them in your head. If you're a first-time seller, it may be helpful to write them down in a journal or a notes app on your phone. You will NOT share these publicly. This is simply an internal guide for you as a seller.

BOUNDS	DEFINITION
Maximum Satisfaction	This is the ideal offer. It can be what you paid for it, the fair market value or anything above.
Optimal Satisfaction	This is the list price that you've already discounted from the original or purchase price. You've determined an acceptable level of satisfaction to sacrifice so that you'll still be optimally satisfied if you sell at that price.
Upper Bound	The upper bound is below optimal satisfaction. It anticipates an offer that requires you to give up more satisfaction than your list price.
Zone of Agreement (ZOA)	The ZOA is somewhere between the upper and lower bounds, in which both parties are willing to compromise.
Lower Bound	The lower bound is a floor beneath which you will reject any offers. It is NOT a "bottom line" price. If an offer is at or near the lower bound, you may accept, counter or decline.

Examples

Let's look at some examples to illustrate how the bounds and ZOA work. I also refer you back to chapter eight, figure 8.3, in which I showcase a real life offer and counteroffer. Below I've also enclosed photos of negotiations, which I handle in bundle chats. In both scenarios, we closed at prices that were within our ZOA.

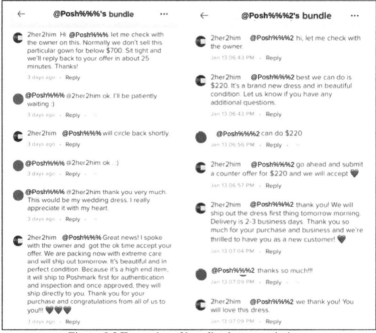

Figure 9.2 Examples of bundle chat negotiations.

Scenario 1

I list a pair of shoes for $250 that I originally bought for $300. They've been sitting in my closet for two months and I've never worn them (hence the $50 discount). My upper bound is $220, my lower bound is $180. Let's say I get an offer for $50. Since that is way below my lower bound, I decline.

A week goes by, and I get a second offer for $185. This is within the ZOA and just slightly above my lower bound. It's high enough that I don't have to decline but it's low enough that I may not want to accept right away. If the shoes are a limited collector's items, for example vintage Air Jordans or the self-lacing *Back to the Future II* Nike shoes, they're rare and hard to come by. If they're common and on sale at your local shoe store, they're easy to get. Think of the circumstances and your personal considerations. I can accept the $185 or I can counteroffer for a little higher, say $200. There's room to negotiate and I can try to get a price more centered within my ZOA. The buyer may decide to counter my counteroffer at a price that's lower but higher than the original offer (e.g., $190) or they may walk away. Don't feel bad if they decline. Knock that FOPO out of your head. If it doesn't work out, move on, and wait for the next buyer.

Let's say the person walks. Two days later, I get a bid for $210. It's lower than my sell price so I'm giving up a little satisfaction but it's close enough to my upper bound that I think it's worth it. I sell and everyone is happy or adequately satisfied.

Alternately, let's say the shoes don't sell. A day goes by, then a week, then a month. This is when FOPO may set in. In the interim, you can continue promoting the item by sharing at Poshmark parties and highlighting them in your stories. As briefly discussed in chapter seven, and as we'll cover in greater detail in chapter 12, items you list on Poshmark can continue to generate SEO juice by your investment of time and engagement on the app. In other words, don't treat listings as static artifacts that are forever tethered to the time you posted them. Continue growing your followers by being proactive within the Posh community and sharing your listings regularly. See each listing as a seedling. Continue to water it, feed it; give it some love and attention, and new offers will eventually spring up as a result. In our experience, we've had new offers come in right away and other times, we've had to wait several months or even a year.

Scenario 2

I decide to sell a suit on Poshmark, which I originally paid $1,400 for. I've worn it a few times but kept it in good condition. I list it for $1250. I decide my lower bound is $900 and my upper bound is $1100. I get an offer for $1050. Even though the offer is the same amount lower ($200) as the first $50 offer I declined for the shoes in scenario 1, the two negotiations are completely different as the suit is a higher priced item. I can work with this and either accept or counter since the offer is within my ZOA. In this case, I would probably accept since it's close to my upper bound.

As the two scenarios illustrate, you can use guideposts when negotiating. Your gut can be helpful too once you gain more sales experience. Just don't use it to accept something that won't satisfy you as a seller. In other words, don't fall into the FOPO trap or seller's remorse. If it helps, write down your bounds and ZOAs as you begin listing items on Poshmark. Eventually, this will become second nature and you'll be able to negotiate with confidence and satisfaction.

- **EXERCISE 1: The ZOA exercise.** Develop your negotiating muscles. We're going to build off the exercises we did in chapter five with more detailed information. Take two or three of your listings and figure out the **ZOA** for each. The ZOAs have two lines to write in ballpark figures.

Item 1	
• Original price	
• Age and Condition	
Pricing	
• Original price (max satisfaction)	
• Sell price (optimal satisfaction)	
Upper bound	
• ZOA	
• ZOA	
Lower bound	

Item 2	
• Original price	
• Age and Condition	
Pricing	
• Original price (max satisfaction)	
• Sell price (optimal satisfaction)	
Upper bound	
• ZOA	
• ZOA	
Lower bound	

Item 3	
• Original price	
• Age and Condition	
Pricing	
• Original price (max satisfaction)	
• Sell price (optimal satisfaction)	
Upper bound	
• ZOA	
• ZOA	
Lower bound	

- **EXERCISE 2: The negotiation simulation.** Below you'll be simulating a negotiation based on a listing with a price and specific conditions. Each choice will lead you to an outcome. Review the item, its condition, and pricing information.
    - **Item:** a leather jacket / **Original price:** $800 / **Age and condition:** five years, has some creases and a few frays in the lining but otherwise in excellent shape / **List price:** $600.
    - **Offer:** $300, IF you:

1.   **Accept** go to 2. **Counter** go to 3. **Decline** go to 4.

2.   Congrats! You sold the jacket for $300. Your earnings come to $240. Later that day, a friend asks if you still have the jacket and is willing to pay $350 for it. Write down how you feel and any thoughts or takeaways.

     _____

3.   The offeror declines. You don't get any new offers and the jacket stays listed for a while. Write down how you feel and any thoughts or takeaways

     _____

4.   The offeror comes back with a $330 counteroffer, IF you:
     •   **Accept** go to 5. **Decline** go to 6.

5.   Congrats! You closed the sale. Write down how you feel and any thoughts or takeaways.

     _____

6.   The jacket doesn't sell and stays up there for a while. Write down how you feel and any thoughts or takeaways.

     _____

Confused? There is no "right" or "wrong" answer. Negotiating is an imperfect science, and everyone will have a different outcome depending on their choices. The point of this exercise is to better gauge your satisfaction levels as a seller. Understanding this will help you make better decisions as you engage in sales and negotiating offers.

Reminder: as mentioned in chapter eight, Poshmark has recently added a "match buyer's last offer" enhancement to counteroffers or what I call a "boomerang" option. Once you counter an offer, if you change your mind, you can replace it with a new one that matches the buyer's last offer.

10 "ALL SALES FINAL" MEANS A HIGHER LEVEL OF RESPONSIBILITY

Now that we've covered the ins and outs of transactions, I'd like to share some of our best tips for shipping and customer communication. In chapter two, I shared why finding the right platform is vital but will not guarantee success. What makes or breaks your success is the service you give to your customers.

In contrast to Amazon and other sales platforms, Poshmark is more seller protective. Generally, all sales through Poshmark are final, whether the buyer accepts the item right away or waits the three-day inspection period. The one exception is if there's a major problem with the item; specifically, that it does not match the description or is severely damaged.

Therefore, it is on you as the seller to be upfront about the condition of the item, especially if you're selling used items from your closet. Be transparent and over-communicative about flaws, damage, or scuff marks, both in your description and in your photos and videos.

For new items, you have a responsibility to communicate with prospective buyers and answer questions in a timely manner and as thoroughly as possible. For my dad's business, this means fielding lots of questions about sizing. Even though sales are final, you don't want to sell something that's not going to fit the buyer. You won't last long as a seller if you do. As I covered in chapter eight, we've sometimes cancelled sales when we knew a buyer was on the fence after hitting purchase or when we knew it would not be a great fit. I'll give another example to drive the point home. After a year on Poshmark, we started listing expensive wedding gowns. I was skeptical as to whether anyone would ever want to purchase gowns online without trying them on. To my surprise, we've since sold quite a few and it's a thrill to be a small part of someone's special day. Each sale has generated significant revenue but comes with a higher degree of care and responsibility.

One time, we had a customer who wanted to buy an expensive wedding gown we had listed that was a size 28. She asked us lots of questions and let us know that she was a size 14. She really loved this specific dress, but we let her know that we only had the one in 28. Because the dress was too big to display on a mannequin, we used catalog photos to showcase it while describing it as a size 28, and tagging it accordingly in the size menu.

Even after our reply, the customer went ahead and made an attractive offer. It was well within the ZOA and close to the upper bound. However, this offer immediately raised a red flag. No, not the scam kind but a wholly different one. This customer was about to buy a gown that was way too big. If she were an in-person customer, she would have clearly seen that the gown wasn't a great fit. However, because she only had the listing photos and really loved the dress, she made an offer without thinking it through. We asked her if she really wanted to buy a size 28 and she asked if it could be altered. As I've learned working with my dad, alterations are generally best if within a one-to-two size margin. Anything more and you're asking for trouble. In this case, a 28 cannot be sized down to a 14. It's just not possible. Even though her offer was spot on, and we would have cleared a lot of money, we declined her offer and politely explained that the dress was too big and cannot be altered to her size. If she had purchased it, she would have been a very unhappy bride stuck with a dress that she couldn't wear. She wouldn't have been able to return it either because it was clearly listed as a size 28, so the customer had full disclosure.

In this case, our responsibility to a customer's happiness outweighed the short-term gain we would have seen from that sale.

Afterward, we updated the description with a more explicit statement that the dress is a size 28 and that the photos are simply representative of style. This was a great teachable moment for us and a reminder to be over-communicative in listings.

The ecosystem protects buyer and seller

In chapter six, I explained why you should not respond to messages that invite you to transact outside the Poshmark ecosystem. One big reason is to ensure that your sales are conducted in a safe and legitimate manner and that you get your money!

For example, let's say a buyer submits an offer and you accept. If the person has a payment issue such as insufficient funds, an out-of-date credit card, etc., Poshmark will halt the transaction and inform the buyer. You don't have to do anything. The buyer will have 24 hours to update their payment method so the transaction can go through. Within that period, the buyer may decide they don't have enough funds or cannot buy at this time, in which case the item goes back on the market for sale. This is one of the ways in which the ecosystem protects you as the seller. It also shields you from awkward conversations with the buyer about payment issues.

How to stand out as a Poshmark seller

Below are the simple rules we adhere to that allowed us to hit the five-figure revenue benchmark in our first year. They aren't hard to follow and yet, you'd be surprised how much this will make you stand out compared to other sellers. Some of these I've covered earlier but they're worth repeating.

- **Communicate with your buyer:** Confirm the shipment of the item and thank them for their business.

- **Don't push your buyer to accept or leave a review / rating:** If the buyer doesn't accept the item immediately after receiving it, don't panic or assume anything. The buyer has a three-day inspection period. Whether they decide to accept early (and thereby release the funds early) or take the entire inspection period, is entirely up to them. Once the three-day period passes, the funds will be transferred into your account on the fourth day. Similarly, don't push a buyer to leave a rating or review. If a buyer is happy with the purchase and wants to express it, they will do so.

- **Don't promise delivery dates:** You can't guarantee when a package will arrive in front of a buyer's doorstep. You can only inform the person that you shipped out the package and provide general guidelines. While USPS priority shipping is generally two to three days, sometimes it may take longer, especially in recent times. You can't control if there's a delay, so don't promise what you can't.

- **Be prompt with sending out orders:** While you can't control when a package will arrive, you can control when you ship it out. To stand out as a seller, be timely in sending out your orders. Try to get your packages to the post office the same or next business day. If you wait too long, Poshmark will cancel the transaction, and no one will be happy. As discussed earlier, take advantage of USPS locations with after-hours drop-offs. You can also schedule pick-ups if you're too busy to get to a USPS location.

- **Pack with care:** Whether big or small, treat each sale as if it were your first and your biggest. Take a moment to remember how you felt when you first sold an item and got a positive review. Pack items with care and do the gratitude exercise covered in chapter eight with each sale.

- **Take photos post-sale:** Take photos of a sold item before you ship it out and of the package once it's sealed and labelled. Save these into a "current orders" album. These photos can be your evidence of the item's condition in the event a buyer opens a case after receiving it. After the transaction is complete and the proceeds are released, you can delete the photos.

Selling as a side-hustle or side-business

If Poshmark isn't your full-time gig, you can still communicate and send out packages in a timely manner. You'll just have to be more structured in doing so. Below are some guidelines to make this easier for you.

- **Designate time blocks:** You may not have lots of time during the day, especially if you run a business or have a full-time job, to check Poshmark. Set aside 30 minute or one-hour blocks to check and respond to questions and most of all, respond to buy offers. Early in the morning, lunch time, or right after work / evenings are good times.

- **Create a work-friendly workflow:** If you're doing this as a side-hustle, your lunch break may be the optimal time to take packages to the post office. Figure out where the nearest post office is from your home or office and decide which is the better and more convenient location. Ask if they have an after-hours drop off slot for packages if you're taking them after work. Designate time blocks within your workday or afterward, to drop off shipments. You can also speak with your postal carrier to see if they can pick up packages from you while delivering your mail.

- **Try to devote at least 30 minutes a day to your Poshmark business:** You don't have to work on Poshmark 24-7. The key is organization. Carve out time blocks to respond to questions, share items, attend Posh parties, and to pack and ship items.

- **Use the vacation setting:** For those days when you're too busy to devote to Poshmark, use the vacation setting, which will temporarily close your store. People can still browse and post questions, they just won't be able to buy until you come back. Be sure to ship out any pending orders first before you "close up shop" for a few days. It's not just for when you actually go on vacation but a way to put on the brakes for when life gets in the way. We'll cover this more in a later chapter when we explore administrative features.

And yes, you can have a successful Poshmark business even if you're busy with a fulltime career. I'll cover this more in chapter 12.

- **EXERCISE:** As you continue listing and sharing items, make sure you are replying to questions in a timely manner. If you're doing Poshmark as a side-hustle, do a time audit of your schedule to identify pockets of time to allocate to it. You may also want to find out where your nearest post office is and take a visit: see if they have an after-hours drop off slot or ask if your regular mail carrier is willing to pick up packages. Introduce yourself and be nice!

11 COMMON POSHMARK INTERACTIONS (AND WHAT THEY MEAN)

Now that we've covered the ins and outs of sales, negotiations, and preparing shipments, let's take a close look at common interactions on Poshmark and what they mean.

As you build up your store with new listings, you'll notice buyers and sellers interacting with them and you. Here are some common interactions.

Likes

Similar to a social media post, Poshmark members can "like" an item by clicking the heart icon. A like can mean that a person is considering buying your item or it could simply mean they are window shopping. For buyers, likes act as bookmarks as they may be browsing hundreds or thousands of items. For sellers, likes can serve as market feedback on items they've listed and potential sales opportunities. For example, if you list an item for $150 and you want to run a one-day sale for $130, you can offer it exclusively to its likers. We'll cover sales in greater detail later in this chapter.

Bundle

Below the like button, is a shopping bag icon. Clicking on it puts an item into a virtual shopping bag or "bundle." Bundles can hold one or multiple items from a seller. Bundles also enable one-on-one chats between seller and buyer. This is a next level up from a like. Sometimes, people use bundles to select a subset from a large closet. As you grow your listings, you'll find bundling occur more often. A bundle doesn't necessarily mean the person will buy what they've put inside it. They may simply be bookmarking items. You can extend private offers to bundlers to incentivize sales.

Shares

Poshmark users will often share your items to their followers or at Poshmark parties. The share button is next to the comment button and resembles a rectangle of two arrows. Think of sharing as someone saying "Hello, fellow Posher!" As I covered earlier, make sure you thank them by following and / or sharing their items. We'll cover Poshmark parties in a separate chapter.

There's one other type of sharing that's a little more advanced called "styling." This is where you share an item from your own closet to a specific individual. Doing so will automatically create a bundle for the person with the item you've shared. Since this scenario happens more frequently when you have many listings, I'll go into more detail about this in a separate chapter.

Figure 11.1 Examples of likes, comments, shares, and bundles.

Comments

Buyers will often ask questions before making a purchase. The most common questions you'll receive will relate to condition and size. Be timely and specific in answering these, giving as much information as possible. Remember, use extra photos if possible. You may also get asked if you consider offers. Whether you do is up to you. Some sellers will only accept buys and not discount any further. Let the buyer know if and whether you are open to offers.

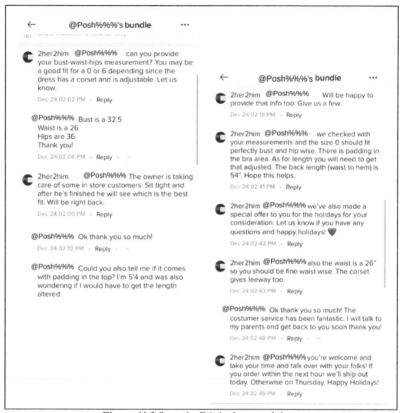

Figure 11.2 Sample Q&A chat on sizing.

Purchase / offers

This is your goal. Someone on Poshmark purchases your item or makes an offer that's within your ZOA. We covered this in chapter nine so go back and review if you need a refresher.

Sales

Over time, you may find that long-term listings are taking up valuable real estate, both virtually and in the real world. Running a sale can help facilitate turning your clothes into cash. For a retail business, Poshmark's sale feature is a great way to move inventory during holidays or other special occasions.

To run a sale:

1. Click "Price Drop."
2. Choose whether the sale is public or limited to item likers.
3. Once you drop the price, Poshmark will notify all likers and give them a 24-hour window to purchase the item at the lower price.

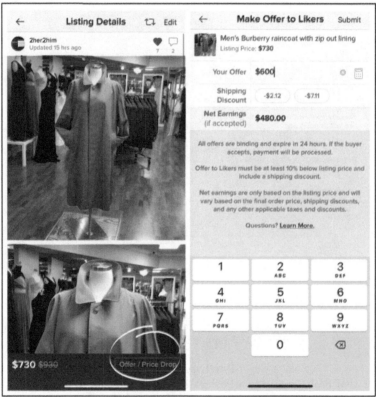

Figure 11.3 Running a sale on Poshmark.

As my dad's Poshmark store started gaining traction in fall 2018, we decided to try a "Black Friday" sale the week of Thanksgiving. We lowered prices on all items the day before Thanksgiving. On Thanksgiving morning, I took my dad to see a movie. By the time the lights came on and the credits rolled, I checked my phone and saw we had seven purchases. We ended up going to the shop to pack and prepare the items to ship out the next day.

Figure 11.4 Building up an appetite for Thanksgiving dinner!

Bulk Actions

If you generate a lot of sales and have multiple items to ship, you no longer have to confirm each one individually. Within "My Sales" under "My Seller Tools," you have an "Actions" menu that will allow you to change the status of all sold items to "Shipped." The seven items we sold in Figure 11.4, we had to confirm individually, one at a time. Now, when we ship more than one item, we can confirm them all at once with the "Actions" menu. You can also use this to download shipping labels.

My Shoppers

In 2021, Poshmark added a feature called "My Shoppers" that allows you to interact with engaged Poshers en masse and generate scale. "My Shoppers" is a sub-menu within "My Seller Tools" and displays all Poshmark users that have interacted with your listings in some way. You can see who has liked, commented, or bundled your items. From there, you can check off one or several users and engage with them all at once to help close more sales. We'll cover this in greater detail when we look at administrative and CRM tools on Poshmark.

BEST PRACTICE TIPS:
- Legit buyers will not ask you to transact outside of Poshmark. Use the red flag to report suspect messages.
- Share the item to a Poshmark handle to open a bundle. Use the bundle chat for negotiations and one-on-one discussions.
- Consider offering a bundle discount (e.g., 10% for two items). You can set bundle discounts within your administrative settings. Bundling allows bulk purchases to be shipped in one package and one shipping cost.
- Use bundle chat rooms to answer questions and negotiate.
- Bundled items will sometimes weigh more than 5 pounds so make sure you have adequate postage by purchasing more as needed (see chapter eight).
- If you make an offer to likers, you can add a shipping discount (either partial or full) that will be deducted from your net sales proceeds.

EXERCISE: As you continue building your store by increasing your listings, study the different buttons and interactions. If you're using Poshmark to buy as well as sell, start looking, liking, and bundling items you may want to buy. Share items when someone shares yours or be proactive and share someone else's listings to start. Answer questions and establish policies and communication protocols for your store. You can do this on the "Meet your Posher" post, which is standard for all accounts. You can also create a separate post with graphics on platforms like Canva (see Figure 11.5).

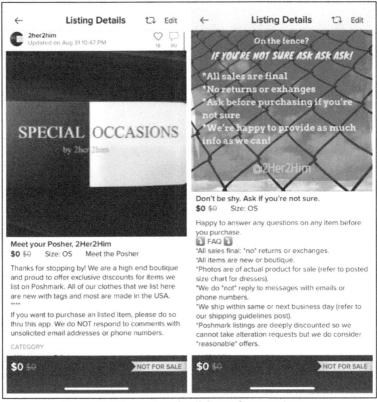

Figure 11.5 Examples of policies and protocol posts.

12 WHAT MY DAY LOOKS LIKE RUNNING A POSHMARK BUSINESS (ON A BUSY SCHEDULE)

Now that you understand some of the virtual "nuts and bolts" to running a Poshmark store, you may be asking if you can really do this with a busy schedule.

Even though my dad's retail store is his primary business, I don't work for him fulltime. I usually spend one day a week at his shop and the rest we do over the phone and text messaging. What is the time commitment for a Poshmark business? It's both an easy and hard question to answer. I'll start by giving you an inside peek into what my average Poshmark day looks like.

Morning

I wake up and hit the gym. While there, I hop on the app (usually while on something that's handsfree like the stationary bike or in-between exercises). I review and respond to questions or make a note to follow-up with my dad if I can't answer them. More importantly, I close sales and negotiate offers. Every morning, we have interactions to go through since prospective customers span the country and different time zones. Questions, offers, etc. often rain in while I'm asleep. **Estimated time: 5 – 15 minutes.**

Throughout the morning, I'll hop on for a few minutes every hour or every other hour, depending on how busy I am. Sometimes, it will be for a few seconds to follow-up on a question or share an item. I often do this when I have a few minutes of downtime (e.g., riding the train or an Uber, waiting for a doctor's appointment, etc.). Think of this as the equivalent of checking Facebook, Twitter, or any other social media account.

Estimated time: 1 – 5 minutes per hour or every other hour.

Mid-day (lunch)

During my lunch hour, I spend a concentrated 10 to 30 minutes responding to messages and offers. If I haven't had a chance to do a morning check-in, I'll make sure to follow-up on questions during this time.

Estimated time: 10 – 30 minutes.

Afternoon

Depending on how busy my afternoons are, I'll continue hopping on for a few minutes every hour or every other hour. Some days, it's easy to integrate into my routine, while others I'm too busy and wait until the evening. Just like social media, spot checks can turn into rabbit holes. The difference is that your Poshmark time is directly correlated with sales and profits.

Estimated time: 1 – 5 minutes per hour or every other hour.

Evening

I spend anywhere from 30 minutes to 45 minutes on Poshmark parties once or twice a week. We'll cover parties more in depth in the next chapter but as a quick reminder, these are designated two-hour blocks during which Poshmark buyers and sellers congregate to peruse and share listings. When we started with just a few listings, I attended parties every day. Now, since we have over 1,000 listings, it takes a lot longer to share all our items. Plus, I'm busier now with other responsibilities. As a result, I have reduced my Poshmark party attendance and focus more on theme-specific ones.

When you start, you may only have a few items in your closet. I encourage you to share out your items and attend as many parties as you can. Five, ten, 50 or even 100 listings won't take you long to share and will gain you greater exposure. The more items you have and share, the more likes, reshares, and comments and questions you will receive. It generally takes me 45 minutes to share most or all the items in our closet and anywhere from ten to thirty minutes to reciprocate share and answer questions.

Estimated time: 30 minutes to 1 hour (for 1000+ listings). If you only have a few items (10 to 50), this will be one to 10 minutes.

Big picture

On average, I spend anywhere from five minutes to one hour a day on Poshmark. The bottom line is that how much time you spend is a function of how big your closet is and how much you can invest in your Poshmark business. If you're super busy with a job, a business (whether clothing related or not), you may want to keep your listings to a select few. Just remember, the more you list, the more seconds and minutes you'll add to your daily Poshmark engagement activities.

There's no precise formula but below is a rough guideline on the number of minutes you'll spend based on the number of active listings you have:

- Time spent checking in the app (minutes) = number of items * 0.005.
- Time spent sharing items at parties (minutes) = number of items * 0.05.
  - Time spent bulk sharing items at parties (minutes) = number of items * 0.027.
- Time spent reciprocal sharing, liking, following at parties (minutes) = number of items * 0.02.
- Time spent answering questions, negotiating sales (minutes) = number of items * 0.008.

To illustrate with some numbers:

Listings	Checking in app (min)	Sharing at parties (min)	Reciprocal sharing, liking, following at parties (min)	Answering questions, negotiating sales (min)	Total	Equivalent
10	0.05	0.5	0.2	0.08	Approx. 1 min.	Browsing a social media app.
50	0.25	2.5	1	0.4	Approx. 5 min.	Watching a short YouTube video.
1200	6	32-60	20-25	9.6	Approx. 40 min to 1 hour.	Watching a TV show or movie.

If you're a numbers geek and want a precise example, I timed how long it takes for me to share 1041 dresses (the number that we have in our closet as of the writing of chapter) using Poshmark's bulk share feature.

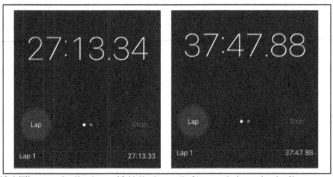

Figure 12.1 Time to bulk share 1041 listings (left); total time, including engagement (reciprocal shares, answering comments) (right).

As you can see from Figure 12.1, the total time, including selecting active listings and sharing took 27 minutes and 13.34 seconds. The second figure adds an extra 10 minutes to account for how long it took me to reciprocal share and follow Poshers who engaged with our listings during that party. As noted above, I used to attend parties every day. Now, I'm more strategic, attending the ones that are most relevant to our closet: in our case, parties related to dresses and "boutique listings." If I have a free moment and there's a party specific to a subset of items such as shoes or jackets and coats, which we have a smaller number of, I'll spend a minute or two to quickly share those out.

The chart above is not a hard and fast formula but a guestimate of how much time to invest based on your inventory. If you have 10 items, you may spend 20 minutes answering questions for a popular item. If you have 500 listings, you may not get any questions on a given day. Remember, time, like anything else, is subject to the quirks and whims of the real world.

If you don't like math, the general rule of thumb is simply the more items you have, the greater the engagement you'll receive, and the more time you'll spend on the app.

While Poshmark may seem like a full-time commitment, many do this as a side gig, and it doesn't require as much time as you may think. One of my former business school classmates, Izzy, is a real estate agent in Florida. She co-runs a Poshmark store with her sister-in-law, Rose. They split up the responsibilities much as I do with my dad. They started in August 2021 with very little social media presence and closed their first three sales within their first week on the platform. Within a month, they hit Ambassador status and continue to make regular sales to this day. My friend, Ashley, who shared the username hack in chapter seven, is another great example. If you think you're too busy to run a Poshmark side gig, Ashley is a third-year med student, wife, and mother of six kids![7] I recently interviewed her for my podcast, and she shared her secret to running a Poshmark store with a simple philosophy that she applies to her life: if it can be done in 30 seconds, do it now. Poshmark is open 24-7, which works for Ashley who doesn't have a normal schedule. She often finds time during the pre-crack-of-dawn hours between 2 am and 4 am to devote to her store. Ashley also leverages her kids to help create listings, like, share and follow other Poshers. Remember, this is a business that you can tailor to your schedule, not the other way around.

Finally, I have to address an elephant in the closet. Since Poshmark is one of my most used apps, I see a lot of social media advertisements for "Poshmark assistants," bots, plugins, or paid services that will share items out for you. Some sellers swear by them and claim they're effective at getting results. For the record, we do not use third-party services, assistants, or bots. The reason is three-fold. First, since Poshmark accounts contain sensitive information, we treat ours like an online bank account. Second, the terms of service prohibit using plugins or bots that automate activities like sharing on Poshmark. As for virtual assistants, it's a bit of a grey area as to whether they're allowed. Some sellers use them, others avoid them. In the early days, sharing was a large time commitment, and I'll be blunt, sharing items one at a time can be tedious for a large closet. While it may be tempting to outsource to a third-party, weigh the risks carefully. Third, you're eating into your bottom line by paying for services without guaranteed results. We are proof positive that you can generate significant revenue without spending all your time on the app, without a big social media presence, and without using external services or plugins. That's just my two cents. We don't have the biggest closet and we don't have the greatest number of sales, but all our success has been through the time we put into the business. Finally, Poshmark continues to add updates to make running your store as user-friendly and time friendly as possible. Bulk sharing is something I advocated for in several Zoom calls I had with people at Poshmark while researching this book. And while I wish I could take credit for it, I can't because I was hardly the first or only one who suggested this. The fact that it was one of the most requested features led it to becoming a reality in late 2021. As I'm revising this chapter, Poshmark just added a "select all" option for bulk sharing, which will make it even more time efficient. Poshmark continues to evolve, adapting to what sellers and buyers want and need. I'm all for hacks and shortcuts so long as they don't risk your store or standing. Instead, let Poshmark know how to do better. Send them an email or tweet at them so they can improve or solve a pain point in future upgrades. A platform is only as good as the community it serves.

- **EXERCISE:** Map out your day. If you're juggling a fulltime job or other responsibilities, identify pockets of time to be active on Poshmark. It only takes a few minutes. If you're tight on time, prioritize answering questions and attending one or two Poshmark parties a week.

13 POSHMARK PARTIES, AMBASSADORS, HOST PICKS, AND CAMPAIGNS

Poshmark parties

In the last chapter, you learned that parties are an important part of my Poshmark schedule. This was my biggest lost opportunity when I started on the platform. If you're new, you may be wondering what the heck is a "party." In the beginning, I got daily notices about these, and I had no idea what they were. I ignored the invites, picturing virtual chatrooms with pixelated cake and punch. It wasn't until six months later that I started engaging in "Posh parties" and today, they're a regular part of my weekly routine.

Poshmark parties are designated two-hour blocks that occur every day, four times a day.

- Themed Parties:
    - o   12 pm to 2 pm ET
    - o   3 pm ET to 5 pm ET
    - o   7 pm to 9 pm ET
- General Parties:
    - o   10 pm to 12 am ET

During these two-hour blocks, buyers and sellers congregate to share items, shop, and sell. Unlike other times on Poshmark, in which people may be browsing or doing individual searches, parties are centered around themes that draw buyers and sellers. Parties sound nebulous but are straight forward events. As a seller, you share items in your closet that fit the party's theme, which are then displayed inside virtual showrooms. Buyers enter those showrooms to see which items have been shared. Unlike other times when you share your listings to your followers or to the Poshmark sea at large, parties are concentrated events. The participants browsing the showrooms are specifically interested in a type of garment or brand.

Themes can be item or brand specific. There are parties for suits, shoes, men's wear and of course, dresses. There's even a party for "boutique" items, which we covered earlier. During these blocks, buyers browse while sellers showcase what they have that fit the party's theme. Think of it as a crowdsourced, online flea market. But instead of setting up a table in a parking lot, you're doing all of this from your phone.

Let's take a closer look at the two types of parties: 1) theme-specific and 2) general.

Figure 13.1 Poshmark party invitations and alerts.

Theme parties

Theme parties occur during the first three-time blocks. They are limited to specific types of clothing, brand names, or specialty items such as home goods, pet goods, or electronics. During theme parties, you can share any item in your closet that fits the theme, which is based on how you categorized them during the listing process.

General parties

By contrast, general parties are open events, in which you can share any item in your closet. They occur during the last block at 10 pm EST / 7 pm PST.

Participating in parties

I recommend keeping the alerts turned on for parties. You'll often see notices for upcoming ones in your app's feed, which you can RSVP to, though it's not required. Once a party begins, you'll get a notification asking if you want to attend. If you click "Yes," you'll be taken to a list of party showrooms. If you're a buyer, you can browse the listings that are being shared or highlighted by the party hosts.

To get a better idea of party mechanics, take a look at the chart below. For buyers, follow the steps in Figure 13.2 to browse. Parties have multiple "showrooms," including main and host picks where you can "window shop."

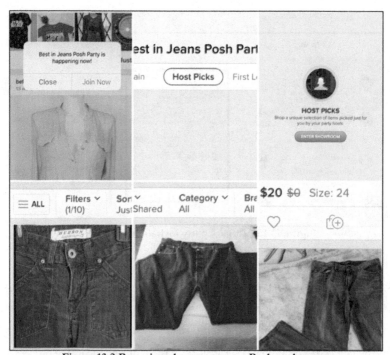

Figure 13.2 Browsing showrooms at a Poshmark party.

For sellers, follow the steps in Figure 13.3 to share and repeat as appropriate, depending on how many listings you have in your closet that fit the party theme. Below, I outline my steps for party sharing, including my power-sharing tip.

- For general parties, you can share everything in your closet. For theme-specific parties, you can only share items that fit the theme. The app will prevent you from sharing an item that doesn't match (e.g., sharing shoes at a coats party).

- If you have a small closet, you should be able to quickly eyeball which items you can share.

- If you have a large closet, I recommend narrowing down your closet by specific brand or item category. This is done by using the funnel button ▼, located towards the top-right of your closet, which will open a menu. Select as many criteria as applicable to the party (e.g., "dresses, suits and skirts" theme party). This will narrow your closet down to those items.

- To share an item to a party, simply hit the share button ↻ underneath a listing and you will see two options: 1) share to the party or 2) your followers. You can always share items to your followers. Click on the party to share it to the event while it's under way. This will send it to the party.

- My power-sharing party tip is to continue scrolling down your list of items and share each one. For the moment, ignore the notifications of people who are liking, commenting, or resharing your items. Focus on sharing everything that fits the party first.

- Avoid sharing items you've already sold.

- Once you've shared everything, go to your news feed, and turn your attention to the people who have liked, followed, and shared your items.
  - Go through and share some of their items to show your thanks.
  - Like any items that catch your attention (if you're a buyer).
  - Follow any Poshers you want to follow.

o   If you see a new Posher with only a few items in their closet, do them a solid and spend a few extra seconds sharing everything in their closet.

As mentioned, Poshmark recently added a bulk sharing option, which next to video is my favorite feature. In the past, sharing 1000+ listings took me about an hour, manually going through and power sharing each one as described above. I still recommend individual sharing if you have a small closet for reasons I'll share in a little bit. However, if you have several hundred or thousand listings, it's a lot of work on your fingers to do this, and it's time consuming.

At the top right of your closet, you'll see a tool icon. Within the menu, you'll see a section called "Bulk Listing Actions." I'll cover this more in depth in a later chapter. For now, the bulk action you want is "share to party."

With bulk share, you can check off which items to share to a party from your closet that fit the theme or item category. You can also use the new "select all" option. Poshmark will automatically filter down to the items that fit theme parties. For general parties, all listings are shareable. You can also bulk share to your followers at any time.

This has cut down the amount of time I spend sharing all our listings by almost half. Instead of hitting the share button for each item and scrolling through the list, I simply select the relevant items that are curated by Poshmark and share.

I do recommend prior to bulk sharing, filter listings to those that are currently available. This will eliminate those that are already sold or not available.

One other important tip. Bulk sharing only works if you're in the app. If you exit out of Poshmark, bulk sharing won't continue. Instead, it will remain stuck on the last item shared and pick up where you left off when you return. I recommend during party hours that you temporarily shut off any auto lock settings on your phone if you have a large closet. You can put your phone aside as Poshmark bulk shares.

Finally, as I mentioned earlier if you have a small closet, I still recommend sharing listings one at a time rather than by bulk share. The reason is that there is a slight trade off with bulk share. I've observed that immediate engagement is lower with bulk sharing than if I share one item at a time. If you have only 10 items, you're more likely to get likes, follows, and questions if you share individually than with bulk sharing. For larger closets, bulk sharing is definitely a huge time saver. The engagement might be less in the short-term, but it will keep your listings fresh and SEO rejuvenated, which will lead to more sales in the long-term.

By following the above steps, you'll develop great Posh friendships and gain new followers. The more you do this, the more likely you are to get offers and sales.

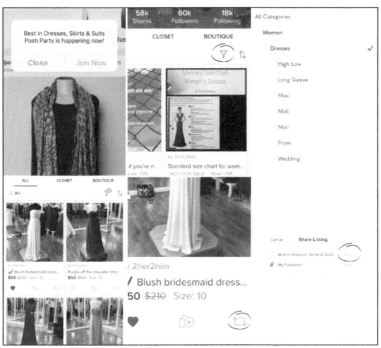

Figure 13.3 Sharing at Poshmark parties.

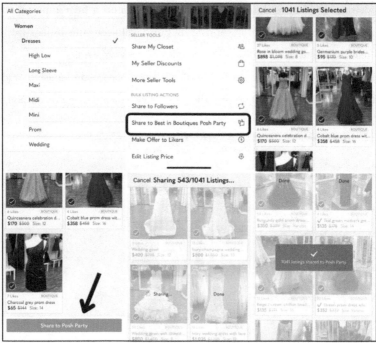

Figure 13.4 Bulk sharing.

As covered in the last chapter, Poshmark parties can take anywhere from a few minutes to an hour, depending on how many listings you have and whether you're bulk or one-off sharing. When you start out, you may have only four or five active listings. Sharing them out will take a minute or less so I encourage you to attend as many parties as you can. As you grow your listings, it will take longer to share all of them at parties.

Host picks

Parties are "hosted" by two or three Poshmark sellers or individuals who work for the company. As you engage in Poshmark parties, you may find some of your items will be selected as a "host pick." Hosts monitor the party showroom and see all the items that are shared during the party. From there, they will select items from different sellers, which are then categorized as "host picks," and placed into a "host picks" showroom.

If you have an item that gets picked as a "host pick," congrats! This means you're selling something that stands out. You'll see that host pick items often get likes, comments, and shares, especially from other Poshers that are participating in the party. Some sellers will update the listing's title to indicate that it's a host pick item. Whether you do is entirely up to you. Either way, having one of your listings earmarked as a "host pick" can help bring greater visibility to your item and store.

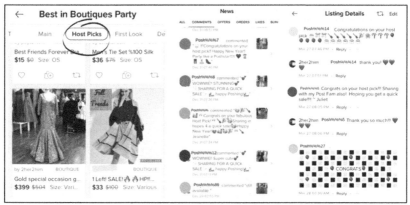

Figure 13.5 Host picks showcase during a Poshmark party.

Hosting Poshmark parties

As mentioned, Poshmark parties are often hosted by Poshmark sellers, typically those with a lot of experience who are plugged into the community. If you check the Poshmark website and blog, you can find out how to volunteer as a party host. Poshmark is constantly updating its platform to integrate social and community-based features like party hosting. Although I haven't hosted one, they can be great opportunities to better understand the platform and learn about trends.

Poshmark ambassadors

Now, let's look at some advanced Poshmark features. First, you may run across sellers that brand themselves as "Poshmark ambassadors." What the heck is an "ambassador?" Whenever I hear that word, I picture someone who looks like the Monopoly man wearing a sash and crown. As we started building our online business, I learned that it's a program for sellers that have achieved several milestones. It's akin to being verified with a blue dot on Twitter or Instagram. Ambassadors are sellers that have accomplished a very specific list of tasks. Once you complete these, you will be invited to join the program. The advantage of being a "Poshmark Ambassador" is that you will be notified of upcoming features early. Moreover, your closet will be recommended to new users, thus increasing your follower and potential customer base. In addition, there are intangible benefits such as being seen as a trusted seller.

Below are the current requirements as of the writing of this chapter:

- 5000 or more shares from your closet.
- 5000 or more shares of other Poshmark sellers' items.
- 50 or more shares of new posher items.
- 50 available (for sale) listings in your closet.
- 15 sales minimum.
- 4.5-star average rating as a seller.
- 3 day or less average ship time.
- 1 "love note," which is a high rating.
- 1 review for an item you purchased on Poshmark.

Figure 13.6 Poshmark ambassador requirements.

To see the current requirements, click into your dashboard and "My Posh Stats."

At first glance, the list looks daunting. When we started, I never thought we'd hit all of the criteria. However, we accomplished them by late fall of our first year and have been in the program since.

Being a Poshmark Ambassador is certainly a nice perk and will help you build visibility and credibility with buyers. However, it's important not to see it as an end all, be all. If you don't hit the criteria, which is admittedly a lot, don't worry. You can still have a successful store and sell many items regardless of whether you participate in the program. Don't make becoming an ambassador a goal. If you're proactive and do the things we've talked about, then you will eventually get there. Also, if you use Poshmark strictly for selling and don't use it to buy (one of the requirements is leaving a positive rating and review for a satisfactory purchase), then it may not be the right goal for you, and that's perfectly fine.

Becoming an ambassador isn't as important as making your Poshmark store a great shopping experience for your customers. Treat each sale, big or small, as if it was a four-figure sale. As you build momentum, don't take for granted a new sale or five-star review. When you hit your 5th, 10th or 50th sale, take a moment to think back to your first one and appreciate that a new or returning customer is putting their trust in you. Don't obsess over whether you will get enough sales fast enough or enough reviews to become an ambassador. I'll reiterate what I said earlier that I don't think it's a good idea to "shortcut" the process by "loss leading" with low prices that cut into your profit or revenue.

In our experience, most customers won't care if you're an ambassador. So long as you answer questions, ship your items quickly, and put time and care into your store, you will get sales. So long as you provide a great shopping experience, you will get great reviews and happy customers.

Ambassador II

As of 2022, Poshmark has added a new level called Ambassador II. Sellers that are already ambassadors and achieve the following benchmarks each quarter will be earmarked with a gold star, denoting Ambassador II status:

- 4000 or more community shares.
- 50 or more listings sold.
- 4.7 or higher average rating.
- 250 or more new listings created.

Unlike Ambassador I, II requires you hit these goals every quarter. Doing so will give you access to Posh events at free or discounted rates, wider promotion within the app, and priority customer support for your store. Again, keep this in perspective. Your goal isn't to get a red or gold star. Your goal is to make sales and provide great service. While ambassador stars are nice accolades, they are more a reflection of the work you put in rather than goals in and of themselves.

Campaigns

Finally, Poshmark has campaigns, which are designed to leverage your other social media accounts to advertise Poshmark as a buying and selling platform. This is available to Poshmark Ambassadors who have connected their social media accounts to their stores (Facebook, Twitter, Instagram). Incidentally when you hit the share button on a listing, you have the option to send it to a connected social media account. Campaigns are curated social media posts created by Poshmark that can generate affiliate revenue for those who post these to their social media accounts. These are available to ambassadors who connect a social media channel with 5000 followers or more. To access these, simply go to your "Account Tab," then "My Seller Tools" and "My Campaigns." Inside, you will see current campaigns and requirements. Each one will have specific metrics and components, including custom tracking links through which Poshmark determines affiliate revenue.

If you're an ambassador with a large following on Facebook, Instagram or Twitter, then connecting your Poshmark store to your social media accounts can give you an even bigger customer base. However, unlike other sales platforms where this is practically a must, you don't have to have a big social media presence to generate sales. We've managed to build up a five-figure business without a large social media following. Moreover, by engaging in parties, we've had fellow Poshers share out our listings to their followers, both on Poshmark and outside of it.

Poshmark campaigns are another opportunity for influencers or those who are highly active on social media.

- **BEST PRACTICE TIP:** Attend theme parties to engage with an item or brand-specific customer segment.

- **EXERCISE:** If you haven't already, attend your first Poshmark party. Share your items, then go back and reciprocate follows, likes, and shares.

You may want to visit the virtual Poshmark showrooms, including the "party room" and "host picks," to see what kind of items are being shared and are trending. Next, look at the Poshmark ambassador and ambassador II requirements. If you've already started selling, see how far along you are. Don't worry if you have a long way to go. Focus on providing a great experience for your followers and potential buyers. You'll automatically make progress towards hitting those benchmarks.

14 INVENTORY MANAGEMENT AND MARKETING

Now that you understand the fundamentals of sales, negotiations, and interactions, let's turn our attention to inventory management, marketing, and how you can combine the two.

Inventory management that doubles as marketing

After we started selling on Poshmark, I learned that one of the most important aspects of my dad's business is inventory management. Since he runs a physical shop, items we list on Posh are also available for purchase in-store. Currently, Poshmark is a self-contained platform with its own inventory and customer relationship management (CRM) system. My dad's shop uses a separate system that does not interface with Poshmark. This means that when we sell an item in-store that we also have listed on Poshmark, we have to take it offline. As a result, we had to get creative and come up with a system to keep track of inventory changes.

Checkmarks (✔)

When we list an item for sale on Poshmark, we use a black checkmark on the item's tag to note that it's listed online. This is my exception to the no emoji rule that I covered earlier. After being on the platform for over a year, we did an inventory audit in winter 2019 to make sure what was listed on Poshmark was still available. With each item that we confirmed, we added a checkmark to the item's tag, indicating that it was listed on Poshmark. For items that we sold in store, we change the Poshmark listing status accordingly. We now use checkmarks on all listings and corresponding tags. This simple manual system helps us keep track of in store items that are listed on Poshmark as opposed to items that we have not yet listed. If a salesperson sells an item with a checkmark, it lets her know that we've also listed it on Poshmark. They can then alert me to update the listing. These extra steps aren't necessary if you're just starting out or if you're exclusively selling online. It's more of a best practice for small businesses using Poshmark as an additional sales channel. Currently, there is no interface or API that connects my dad's point-of-purchase system and Poshmark. I hope Poshmark will create one or adapt its platform to connect with other point-of-purchase systems. This could be a huge game changer if it wants to dominate the small business market. For retail shops, inventory management is a constant challenge. Until then, my work-around uses checkmarks and stock-keeping-unit (SKU) numbers, discussed below.

SKU ("style no. XYZ")

As I covered in chapter three, when we list items on Poshmark, we add a stock-keeping-unit (SKU) marker comprised of a tag's style number or barcode number in the description section. Using a SKU helps us locate it quickly rather than sift through our entire closet. Poshmark recently added a search within your own closet feature, which makes narrowing down even easier. In the past, we would have to run a search-at-large through the entire Poshmark ecosystem, often pulling up results from other closets with similar items or SKU tags. Now, you can search within your own closet using a SKU or a run broad search with a word or phrase.

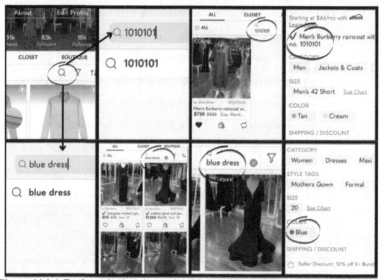

Figure 14.1 A Poshmark closet search with specific and broad search examples.

If you start with a few listings, you won't have to worry about this since it's easy to scan your closet. However, the more listings you add, the more time it will take to browse through all of them. Using a SKU allows you to locate items quickly and the more specific the SKU, the easier it is to find. As mentioned, you can search within your own closet or all of Poshmark. Expanding your search beyond your closet may be helpful to gauge popularity, demand, or item scarcity. You may also get ideas from fellow Poshers on listing best practices.

If we don't have a SKU, we simply create a one and write it on the tag. Poshmark has a separate menu called "Additional Details (Private)," in which you can add a SKU. However, I find it easier and less time consuming to add it to the details section. I use the prefix "style no." + <SKU> (see chapter three).

1. If my dad sells an in-store item that's listed on Poshmark, he texts me the style number or a photo of the tag and I input the SKU in our closet's search bar to locate it.

2. I edit the item, changing the quantity for multiples or updating the availability from "for sale" to "not for sale" for single items.

3. For single items, I also change the title and description, adding "☆SOLD☆" to indicate that it was sold in-store.

You don't have to do this. If you sell or give away an item that you have listed, you can delete it from the app if that's easier. However, changing the status allows us to keep the item displayed in our closet while taking it off the market. It works both as inventory management and marketing. Whether you're running a retail shop or simply cleaning out your closet for extra cash, this technique can be helpful if you sell the item elsewhere or donate it. It's a little extra time on your part but consider using the "not for sale" status to keep it displayed within your store rather than pull it down altogether. Often, we'll get questions on an item that's no longer available, giving us valuable market feedback on what to restock.

Figure 14.2 A Poshmark inventory hack that doubles as a marketing tactic.

Remember, you can also set a listing to drop at a future date. This is a great way to showcase items that you plan to sell by giving buyers a sneak peek ahead of time. Using the "drops" availability status can be a great marketing tool and strategy to pique buyer interest. For more on this, go back to chapter three.

Now, I want to share with you one of my most effective and powerful marketing tactics that we use on Poshmark to generate followers and sales. Ironically, it's one we discovered completely by accident.

Since we use Poshmark as an online channel for a retail store, we take all of our photos at the shop. This helps with branding and consistency. A side effect is that our "photo studio" has clothes everywhere. Inside, mannequins line the back rows and during our Poshmark listing days, my dad and his sales staff spend time dressing the mannequins with the garments that we list. During the photo sessions, as I finish one listing, my dad rotates out mannequins so we can create listings quickly and efficiently. An unintended side effect is that many of the other mannequins are visible in the background of listing photos.

As our store grew, we started getting questions about items in the ***background*** of listings. People would say things like "I love the dress in the back, do you have that one listed?" Or "I really love that outfit, is it for sale?" Often, those items were ones we had already listed or planned to list but hadn't gotten around to yet. When we started, our goal was to experiment with a few listings, much as we did with other platforms. As we gained traction, my dad kept moving the goal post and we increased our listing output. Today, we have close to 30% of the entire store's inventory listed with a goal of eventually putting every item we have online. The reason is simple. Listing it on Poshmark means it's visible 24 hours a day, nationwide.

Additionally, comments provide valuable market feedback. Seeing that a potential customer is interested in an item that's ***behind*** a featured listing helps us prioritize items to list or restock. This tactic has opened the door to more sales and deeper engagement with customers. It was the best kind of "accident."

Figure 14.3 Marketing tactic in action.

Signage

As we gained new followers, increased sales, and our overall Poshmark presence, we quickly discovered that many buyers asked similar questions about sizing, size charts, return policies, shipping dates, etc. To address this, we created signage, which we posted as separate listings to answer frequently asked questions (FAQs). As mentioned throughout this book, my favorite tool to create signage is Canva (www.canva.com). Canva is user-friendly with both a premium and robust free option with tons of stock photos and text options. You can also upload photos to use as backdrops and create professional looking signage within minutes. Since Poshmark uses square photos, you can use an Instagram template or create your own. We've used Canva to create signs for "Black Friday" and "Cyber Monday" sales, and for when the shop is temporarily closed for vacation or travel (1 will cover this more in a later chapter).

Once you create a sign, list it as you would an item that you're selling using the "other" category combined with the "not for sale" status. Add relevant copy to your headline and description. For seasonal or temporary signs, be sure to pull them down once they're no longer relevant or active.

> ♦ **EXERCISE:** Develop your inventory management system whether it's checkmarks on the tag or your own numbering system (especially if there is no tag). Even if you only have a few items, get into the habit early. You'll save yourself a lot of time and headache down the road if you decide to grow your business. Use Canva or another graphics tool to spruce up your store with signage. I recommend creating them in advance, especially for sales, vacations, holidays, closure periods, and FAQs. Keep them on your phone and repost when needed. Below are some examples of signs I've created for our store. Feel free to crib and / or modify.

Figure 14.4 Examples of signage created on Canva.

15 ADVANCED FEATURES AND ADMINISTRATIVE TOOLS

Now that we've covered the basics, let's look at some advanced features that can really help you manage a Poshmark business.

Drafts

When we started in 2018, I was working with my dad at his shop once a week and often, he would be pulled in multiple directions, interrupting our listing process. During those times, I would exit out of the app, hoping that my listing was preserved in some mid-creation ether when I came back to it. The problem was that sometimes the app would reset, and I'd lose my place. Moreover, I wasn't able answer other alerts such as comments or offers. I would either have to finish the listing or cancel it. In 2019, Poshmark added a drafts feature. If you're in the middle of creating a listing and need to close it midway, the app will ask if you want to save it as a draft. The next time you create a listing, you will see a link to a drafts folder at the top-right, which you can click to continue from where you left off.

Styling

In chapter 11, I briefly talked about "styling" as a way to share specific items from your closet to an individual Poshmark user. I'll go over the mechanics in just a bit. But first, let's talk about when and why you might want to do this. In the beginning, you may have just a few listings. When a Poshmark buyer stumbles onto your closet or an individual listing, they may start exploring your entire catalog to see what else you offer. That's easy to do when you have a small number. But as you grow your business and expand listings into triple or quadruple digits, that becomes time consuming and cumbersome. Alternately, you may have a buyer who loved an item they purchased from you, had a great shopping experience, and wants to see what else you sell. They may ask you for guidance or suggestions. We've gained a few repeat customers during our time on Poshmark, and they are among the most valuable relationships to cultivate.

As we grew our listings to 1400+, we got more posts from potential customers asking for guidance. For example, one Poshmark user posted that she loved a dress but wanted to know if we had it in another color. Some would ask if we had items with specific accouterments (e.g., ruffles, no ruffles, etc.). Others would simply tell us what kind of dress or garment they were looking for.

Again, this occurs when you have a large selection, which is why I include it in this chapter rather than the basic interactions in chapter 11. We only started getting these types of inquiries once our inventory grew to over 100 pieces.

The mechanics of styling are very similar to sharing at parties. Instead of sharing a listing to a party or all your followers, you're sharing to a specific user.

To "style" someone on Poshmark, use the share button ⟳ below the item and type in the Poshmark handle of the person you're sharing it to.

The tricky part about styling is finding those items that a buyer is looking for, especially if you have hundreds or thousands of listings. Since I'm not a clothing or style expert and my dad is often busy, I learned how to "style" using a simple set of procedures.

- **Communicate.** Ask for the basics: size, color, garment type, specific features (e.g., short or long dress or name brand), and a budget or cost range. A customer may add some of their own criteria as well.

- **Select.** Go into your closet and choose a specific item or use the filter button ▼ to narrow down to a subset (see chapter 13 for a review).

o **Share.** Hit the share button and type in the Poshmark handle of the buyer. For additional shares, you will see the individual listed as the first option after your first share so you can click on their profile instead of typing the handle every time.

- **Bundle.** Sharing an item to a user will create a bundle, in which the buyer can inspect, comment, purchase, or tender an offer.

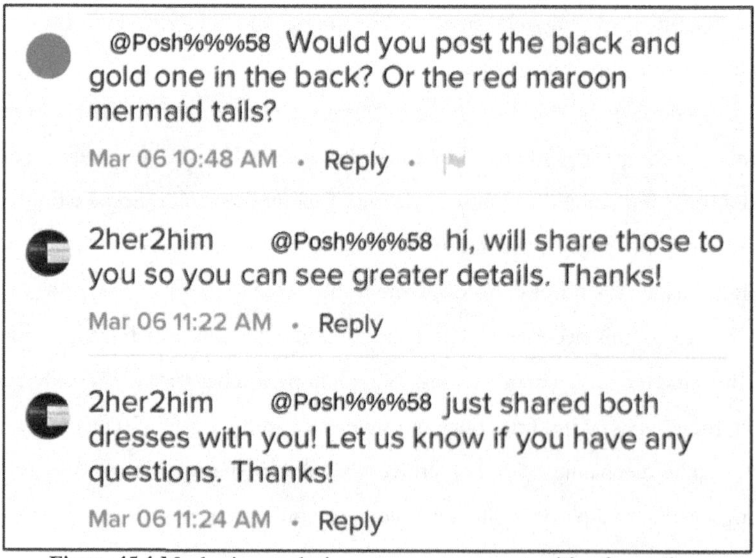

@Posh%%%58 Would you post the black and gold one in the back? Or the red maroon mermaid tails?

Mar 06 10:48 AM · Reply ·

2her2him   @Posh%%%58 hi, will share those to you so you can see greater details. Thanks!

Mar 06 11:22 AM · Reply

2her2him   @Posh%%%58 just shared both dresses with you! Let us know if you have any questions. Thanks!

Mar 06 11:24 AM · Reply

Figure 15.1 Marketing technique to create opportunities for styling.

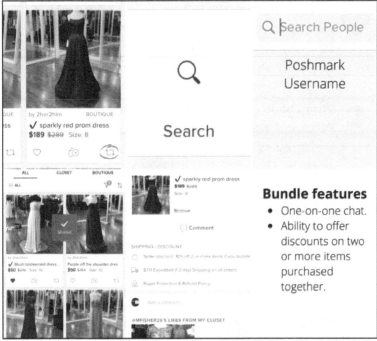

Figure 15.2 Styling on Poshmark.

When it comes to styling, don't be pushy or aggressive. A pet peeve of mine is when sellers start styling me out of the blue, especially since we're primarily a seller, not a buyer. Don't style without a clear indicator or prompt. If a potential customer wants your help, they will ask. I often ask the person if they would like suggestions before sending items. Most of the time they are receptive and welcoming. If you're not sure just ask.

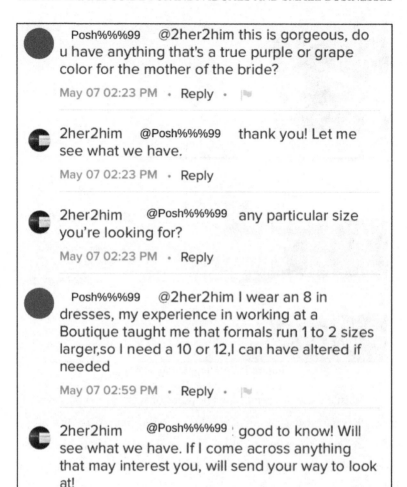

Figure 15.3 Inquiries are opportunities to style.

Stories and video

We've covered video and stories in chapter four. Video has been a long-requested feature and I encourage you to use it as part of your branding and marketing efforts.

As a reminder, stories will automatically link to your closet and can be liked or reshared by others. It's a great way to replicate a social media like experience. Remember, videos in listings will automatically double post within your stories. (See chapter four).

Administrative tools on Poshmark

Now, let's look "under the hood" at some of the important administrative and CRM tools on Poshmark. As discussed, Poshmark takes a commission on sales so it's helpful to know what the platform provides in return for that. Whether you use it to expand an existing retail business or start a side hustle, it's vital that you "maintain your house." The administrative tasks aren't sexy, but they're key to staying organized and keeping your business running and growing.

To access your administrative tools, click on your Poshmark handle at the bottom-right of the screen.

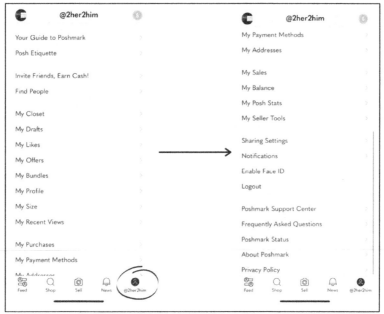

Figure 15.4 Administrative tools menu.

My Payment Methods

If you're buying on Poshmark, you can choose any number of payment methods, including credit or debit card, PayPal, or Venmo. Remember, if you sell and buy, you can apply any sales proceeds within your Poshmark account as a payment method.

My Seller Tools

This is one of the most important sections for sellers. Inside, you'll find a lot of helpful resources, all of which come with your Poshmark account. We've covered the new "My Shoppers" feature which is at the top of the "My Sellers Tools" list. We'll now explore settings for bundle discounts, sales and inventory reports, and more. What makes Poshmark a competitive and attractive solution are its administrative and CRM tools, which are comparable to other platforms that require a monthly subscription fee. Here, you get access to extensive data and analytics without any upfront or standing costs.

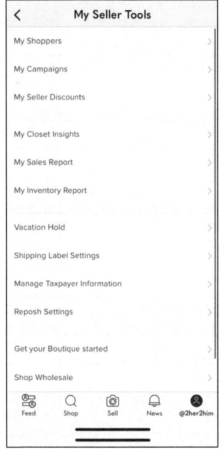

Figure 15.5 My Seller Tools.

1. My Seller Tools: My Shoppers

As briefly mentioned in chapter 11, Poshmark has a section called "My Shoppers" within "My Seller Tools." My Shoppers allows you to get a 10,000-foot view of who has engaged with items in your closet. You'll see a list of items along with users and touchpoints, including likes, comments, bundles. From there, you can select one or more users and engage en masse. Below are the three engagement options available within My Shoppers:

1. **Add Likes to Bundle:** this will create bundles of items for likers.

2. **Send Offer to Bundle:** if a Posher has bundled an item, you can send a discount their way. The discount can be for a single item or added on top of a bundle discount for two or more items. We'll cover bundle discounts later in this chapter.

3. **Send Comment to Bundle:** this allows you to send messages to Poshers that have bundled items. You can engage with a greeting or offer to answer any questions they may have.

These features are a great way to engage with more than one potential buyer, especially if you have a lot of listings. Moreover, if you're using Poshmark for a retail business, you now have tools to expand your reach.

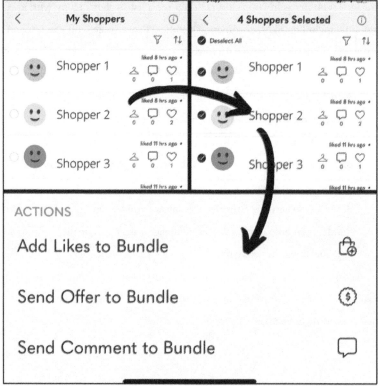

Figure 15.6 My Shoppers.

2. My Seller Tools: My Closet Insights

In addition to My Shoppers, "My Closet Insights" was added in 2021 to give you a look at your shop's performance. With My Closet Insights you can get a quick snapshot "Summary" of sales, net earnings, listings sold, and current orders by period. Next, you can see "Brand Insights" to indicate which brands in your closet are selling. Third, the "Sales Insights" section will display sales stats, which you can filter by demographic. The "Order Insights" section will show trends based on sale type: by "Offer," "Buy Now," "Bundle Offer" or "Bundle Buy Now." Finally, you'll get a quick view summary of new listings you've created, your current inventory, brand sales trends, and listing insights by dollar value. This is an incredibly powerful tool that acts as a dashboard and a performance odometer for your closet.

Figure 15.7 My Closet Insights.

3. My Seller Tools: My Sales Reports

Sales reports allow you to compile and review sales data over a period or date range. You can see how and when items have sold, to whom, and where. As you grow your Poshmark store, start reviewing your sales reports on a regular basis. This will give you a clear picture of how your business is doing and where to invest your time and energy.

4. My Seller Tools: My Inventory Reports

The inventory report will compile a spreadsheet of everything you have actively listed for sale on Poshmark. This is useful if you have a large closet and want to do inventory checks. As I covered earlier, if you're selling on multiple channels, on or offline, you'll have to audit your listings occasionally for accuracy. I reiterate my hope that Poshmark will one day be able to interface with external point-of-purchase and

CRM systems for retail stores. For now, inventory reports are a good tool to review your closet's listings.

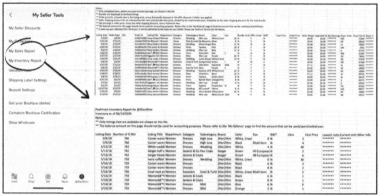

Figure 15.8 Sale and inventory reports.

5. My Seller Tools: Vacation Hold

If you're traveling or taking a break, turn on your vacation settings. This will deactivate your listings, temporarily converting them into a "not for sale" status until you return. Visitors will see a banner letting them know that you are away until a specified date. Of all the administrative features on Poshmark, this is one of the most useful but also one of the most confusing for buyers. The benefit of the vacation setting is that it's a quick and easy way to take your store offline. You can schedule start and end-dates for your vacation in advance or simply take your store offline until you're ready to reopen.

I'm a firm believer that a break is a break. If you keep your store open, it means you're open for business and people have an expectancy that you're going to answer questions, reply to offers, and most importantly, fulfill orders in a timely manner. So, use the vacation setting if you need time away, even if for just a day or two.

The downside of the vacation setting is that it converts your entire catalog into the "not for sale" status. The only notification a buyer sees is a small pop-up if they happen to go into your closet. Whenever we've gone on vacation or used this setting, we inevitably get questions and some panicked comments about an item a person has had their eye on, which is no longer available to purchase. The other downside is that followers and likers don't get any sort of notification or obvious signal that you've returned. I imagine this is to reduce the number of alerts. However, my hope is that Poshmark will update this feature to make it more explicit. One simple solution would be a separate status marker for temporarily offline listings. For example, "on vacation, will return" instead of "not for sale" would be less confusing.

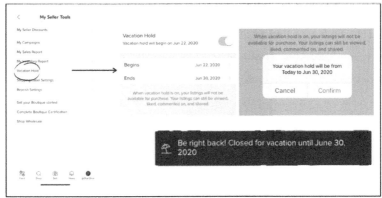

Figure 15.9 Vacation hold.

6.   My Seller Tools: Shipping Labels

Make sure your shipping info is current and up to date, whether you're a buyer or seller.

In 2020, Poshmark added the option to print packing slips with your shipping labels. The packing slips showcase the item purchased with the title and purchase price. This can serve as an additional spot check to make sure you're shipping the correct item.

Notifications

Another section that I recommend you adjust are the notifications and alerts. Do this before you start. When you set up your Poshmark account, by default every notification is turned on. This means you're getting a ding on your phone for everything that happens, including likes and follows. Manage these by switching off alerts and keeping only the ones you need. I turn off the alerts for new followers (those add up fast) and leave on the ones for comments, parties, and bundles, as those are tied to sales opportunities. You can also manage your email settings there.

Sales tax

One thing that Poshmark does well is that it eases some of the burden of managing an online business when it comes to sales tax. As an online retailer, your customers are all over the US, which means that your business will touch many different states. If you're selling a dress to a customer in California, shoes to someone in Florida, and a coat to a buyer in Colorado, the transaction will be subject to that state's sales tax laws. This can be a nightmare if you're using a platform that doesn't take this into account or requires you to manually set each state's tax rate. Poshmark automatically calculates and adds that to each purchase, making it easier for both buyer and seller. It also makes it that much easier for a small business to properly categorize sales from Poshmark.[8]

- **BEST PRACTICE TIPS:**
    - o Follow the person you're styling. When you type their handle into the search bar, it will autofill based on your follow list.
    - o Create signage (see chapter 14) for vacation and closure periods.
    - o Use the Poshmark ambassador checklist to assess engagement levels even if becoming an ambassador is not one of your goals (see chapter 13).
    - o Check "My Closet Insights" on a periodic basis to review how your closet is doing, and get a high-level sales analysis according to brands, trends, and demographics.

- **EXERCISE:** Explore the administrative features, including "My Seller Tools," and "Notifications." Check out "My Shoppers" to find engagement opportunities with potential buyers. Explore "My Closet Insights" to get a big picture of how your closet is doing. Manage your store, generate a sales report, and try the different analytic and CRM options. These tools will become more important as your business grows.

16 TO PARTNER OR NOT TO PARTNER?

Now, let's explore partnering with someone to run a Poshmark business. Throughout this book, I've shared **our** journey; emphasis on "our." You'll recall that my dad and I tried out many e-commerce platforms. Our goal was to make his business more competitive and current. We discovered Poshmark in May 2018 and have since invested more time and energy into it to expand his business.

What does working with my dad look like? Schedule-wise, we meet once a week at his shop, typically Tuesdays or Wednesdays. On those days, we create new listings, averaging anywhere from five to 30 in a given week. We also do inventory spot checks, making sure that what we have listed matches what we have in stock. For a more detailed look at my day-to-day, I refer you back to chapter 12.

The rest of the week, it's all about communication and coordination.

If you're selling on Poshmark as a side hustle, you may be thinking about working with a partner. By partner, I mean someone who shares the responsibilities, expenses, and proceeds of the business with you. The advantages of partnering with someone range from increasing your inventory to doubling your coverage on the app. As I covered in previous chapters, engagement is key: immersing yourself in the community by attending Poshmark parties, sharing listings (yours and others), and answering questions. This leads to sales.

Having been on the app for four years, I believe there are three cornerstones for making a Poshmark partnership work.

1. Communication.

2. Dividing responsibilities.

3. Trust.

Let's take a look at each one in turn.

Communication

As discussed above, my dad and I only work together, in-person, once a week. This means, the rest of the week we communicate through texts and phone calls. As the customer-facing part of the Poshmark business, I handle most of the in-app activities: communicating with potential customers, sharing at Poshmark parties, and negotiating offers. My dad is the subject matter expert. He knows clothes and the nitty gritty details about brands, sizing, cut, and color. When I get a question that I don't know the answer to, I text or call him for guidance. It's a delicate balancing act since we're both very busy. Sometimes, I have to wait for an answer since he's attending to other business. My dad also sets the guidelines for negotiating offers; giving me the guideposts on the ZOA for listings so I can close a sale at a satisfactory price (for more on this, review chapters eight and nine). Communication between partners and to your customers is the foundation for a great Poshmark experience.

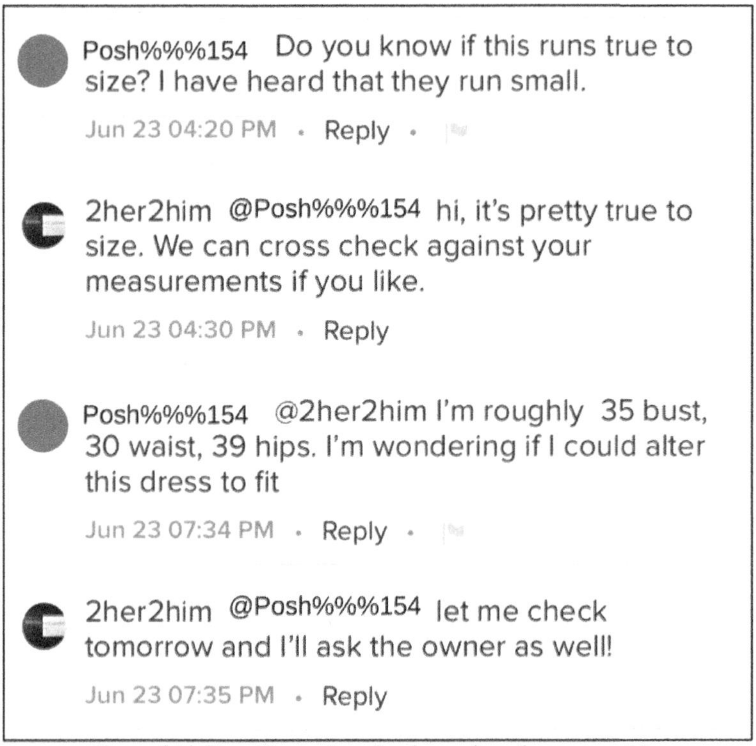

Posh%%%154 Do you know if this runs true to size? I have heard that they run small.

Jun 23 04:20 PM · Reply ·

2her2him @Posh%%%154 hi, it's pretty true to size. We can cross check against your measurements if you like.

Jun 23 04:30 PM · Reply

Posh%%%154 @2her2him I'm roughly 35 bust, 30 waist, 39 hips. I'm wondering if I could alter this dress to fit

Jun 23 07:34 PM · Reply ·

2her2him @Posh%%%154 let me check tomorrow and I'll ask the owner as well!

Jun 23 07:35 PM · Reply

Figure 16.1 Chat illustrating the dynamics of a partnership.

Dividing responsibilities

Dividing who does what is another important ingredient for a successful Poshmark partnership. My dad and I split the responsibilities based on our strengths and expertise. I manage the in-app engagement, while he handles operations and product knowledge. To illustrate, when we close a sale, I let him know that we've sold an item. Even though we're both on the app, I provide extra redundancy by texting him a link of the sold listing. The mailing label goes straight to his email. Since all the inventory is at the shop, he finds the sold item, packs it, prints out the shipping label, and takes it to USPS for shipping. Once that's done, I confirm it on the app and let the customer know we have shipped. We both enjoy what we do. My dad loves the physical packing of the item, printing out the labels, and taking trips to the post office, while I enjoy negotiating and closing sales. This is just one way to divide responsibilities. You and a partner may follow a similar workflow or do a 50-50 split on all activities. Figure out what works best for you by leveraging your strengths, schedule, and what you enjoy doing.

Trust

This is the through line for communication and dividing responsibilities. Whether your partner is a family member, friend, or someone you've decided to work with, make sure you trust one another. If you decide to be partners on Poshmark, you are sharing access to the same store, the same log-in, and the same information, including financials. Treat it as if you're sharing a joint bank account. I hope Poshmark will develop the ability to designate sub-accounts for employees or sales staff, so you can limit their access. Until then, having a partnership based on trust is paramount.

Planning for if the sh*t hits the fan

This is part of the trust factor but important enough that it deserves its own paragraph. When entering a partnership, it's easy to focus on the positive. However, you'll soon discover that any partnership will have its rough spots, misunderstandings, and mistaken assumptions. It's best to discuss these ahead of time and come up with dispute resolution or "if sh*t hits the fan" measures. If you feel uncomfortable doing this, then it's all the more reason to make it front and center of your partnership planning. If you can't discuss problems before they arise, just imagine what it will be like if, and when, they occur. Either get comfortable early on talking about potential problems or save yourself the trouble and don't partner at all. I recommend you talk out your worst-case scenarios: what if partner A fails to ship orders on time or partner B isn't attending parties like they agreed to. How will you resolve these? You should also schedule regular temperature checks by phone, video conferencing, or in person. Discuss what's working and what needs improvement. Finally, discuss the "parting of the ways" scenario. If you end up in "irreconcilable differences" land, how will you end the business? This includes separating inventory, splitting proceeds and expenses. Basically, who gets what in a divorce.

BEST PRACTICE TIPS:

- o If you're not able to answer a question right away, send a quick reply that you will follow up within an hour or as soon as you can.
- o Create standard message templates and put them in a notes app on your phone to copy and paste into replies.
- o Have Poshmark emails forwarded to your business partner's account by creating a rule (e.g., have all emails with the word "Poshmark" forwarded to this address).

EXERCISE: If you're thinking about taking on a Poshmark partner, figure out the logistics and day-to-day responsibilities. Have the hard conversations before you enter into a partnership. How do you handle disagreements and conflicts? How do you divide responsibilities, how do you allocate your time (how much time do you have to allocate)? What do you do if things go south, and you decide to part ways? What's your exit strategy? Finally, figure out how to divide the responsibilities and rewards. Consider all of these issues before you decide to take that Posh leap together. If both of you are investing significant resources, including inventory or capital to purchase inventory, you may want to sign a formal partnership agreement. In that case, it may be a good idea for you to consult with an attorney(s).

- o If you are the owner of a retail business or boutique, map out the responsibilities between you and any co-owners. Determine how you will manage your Poshmark inventory with your in-store items. Decide how you will involve sales staff in helping you run the Poshmark part of the business.

17 SCREW UPS, COMPLAINTS, RETURNS, AND ONE-STAR REVIEWS

Poshmark sounds peachy right? So far, it's been a smooth roller coaster ride with jazzy music in the background. Everything's perfect with easy sales, happy customers, and you'll never have a problem ever again.

Not so fast.

You've read enough into this book to know that I am a fan of the platform. But no platform is perfect, and no seller is perfect. If you sell long enough, you'll occasionally run into problems. The more you sell, the more you grow, and the more you'll sometimes have those not so perfect moments and headaches to deal with. And if I'm being completely candid, I've made some mistakes too. It happens. We're all human. While I believe being a five-figure Poshmark seller is a wonderful thrill, I would be remiss if I didn't include this chapter and let you know about some of the frustrating moments that come with running an online business.

Below, I'll cover some of these difficulties and how to deal with them. I share these not to scare you off but to keep you informed so you can weather the bad times and have more great ones.

Complaints

As covered earlier, when you ship your item, the buyer has three days to inspect it. If there's a problem, the customer may do one of several things.

They may reach out to you

You may receive a message, typically posted as an item comment or in a bundle chat. Recently, Poshmark added a private chat option within sold listings. Buyers can reach out to sellers with a message with their purchase. Sometimes, a buyer will reach out to say thanks or to express their gratitude. They may also use this channel to ask a question or indicate an issue. As I'll cover in greater detail below, be polite, patient, and pleasant when interacting with customers. If the customer has a complaint or an issue that can't be resolved, advise them to open a case. You can also escalate a chat to Poshmark or report it, if need be, by clicking on the three dots.

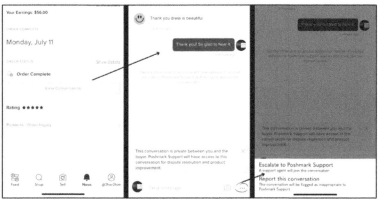

Figure 17.1 Poshmark's new listing chat feature includes the ability to escalate to Poshmark support.[9]

The most common customer comments are:

Wrong size (can I exchange?)

This happens. Even though we encourage people to ask questions and provide their measurements so we can doublecheck sizing, sometimes someone will order a dress or garment and then ask if they can exchange it for a different size. On Poshmark, items can't be returned due to sizing so the best thing to do is politely let them know that you can't accept returns or exchanges. Since many Poshmark buyers are also sellers, you can encourage them to relist and sell it.

Something is missing

One time a customer ordered a dress and upon receipt, she informed us that a belt was missing. My dad assured me that the belt was packed with the dress. However, since it was a cloth belt and we happened to have a spare, we decided to send it to her and cover the postage. This was an easy fix, she was happy with the solution, and gave us five stars. If something like this happens, try to work it out with your buyer. Offer a replacement (and pick up the tab on the shipping), a gift card, or a discount on a future Poshmark purchase. If they're still not satisfied, don't engage in a prolonged back and forth. Simply advise them to escalate it to Poshmark, which will open a case. More on this later.

The listing didn't have the full information

Another time, someone ordered a bridesmaid dress only to discover that it was extra-long and would need to be altered. As I didn't know what an extra length dress was, we didn't disclose it on the listing, and it escaped our attention. The buyer received the dress and let us know that it wasn't as advertised, and she was right. I confirmed with my dad's business partner that this specific dress was extra-long. This is a detail we should have disclosed when we listed it. We let her know she could open a Poshmark case, and that we would support her if she wanted to return it. However, she simply wanted to know if it could be altered. After confirming with my dad that it could, I let her know. She was satisfied with our response and gave us a great rating and review. I can't promise things will always work out this smoothly but if you realize you've made a mistake, own up to it, and support them if they want to return it. On a side note: we updated the listing's description (since we had two of them in stock), disclosing it was extra-long. We later sold the second dress, but this time had no issue because the buyer knew what she was getting.

For the most part, if someone reaches out to you with a problem, they want to resolve it with you. Be polite, patient, pleasant, and do what you can to make things right. If it's your error, own up to it.

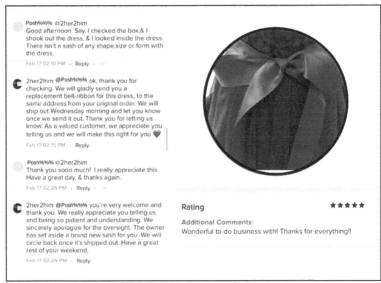

Figure 17.2 Resolving a customer issue.

Case opened

Sometimes, a buyer will not reach out but instead press the report-a-problem button. You'll immediately be notified that they've opened a case. What that means is that the buyer is not satisfied and has appealed to Poshmark. Since all sales are final, Poshmark must review the case and act as a mediator to decide if the complaint merits a return and refund. If you're upfront about your listings, answer questions thoroughly, and ship in a timely manner, most of the time you'll be fine. However, if you sell long enough, you will run across a case from time to time. As of the writing of this book, we've sold over 350 items on Poshmark and the majority of these have been smooth transactions with satisfied customers. That said, we've had a few cases to deal with along the way.

When a customer opens a case, it opens a private chat on Poshmark that is visible only to you, the buyer, and Poshmark. Each side is asked to upload pictures and post statements. Poshmark then reviews the case and makes a final decision. If Poshmark decides in your favor, the case is closed, the transaction is final, and the proceeds are released to you.

If Poshmark decides in favor of the buyer, then the buyer has a small window (two to three days) to ship back the item. Poshmark sends them a return label and once you receive the item, you can inspect it to make sure it is in the same condition as when you sold it. If not, you can file a counter-complaint. Otherwise, the case is closed, and the buyer is refunded their money. If the buyer does not ship the item within the return window, the transaction is closed, and the proceeds are transferred to you. I'll go over a few scenarios below.

Item was damaged

If there's a mark or rip, however slight, it can be the basis for a case. Therefore, you have to be thorough in your listing and disclose any blemishes or flaws, no matter how small. We've had a few instances, in which there was a blemish or popped stitch. In those cases, if it's clear in the picture, we usually just accept it and support the return. In one of the cases, the item was returned, and we re-listed it at a discount, disclosing the blemish. In another, the buyer ended up keeping the item, so the sale closed after her return window expired, and Poshmark released the proceeds. In a third, a buyer ended up dismissing the complaint because he had a change of heart. Despite us supporting his claim since the pictures demonstrated he was correct; he didn't realize that opening a case meant he was asking for a return. He simply wanted to point out a flaw. However, he wanted to keep the item because it was new, and he got a great deal on it.

Item did not match the description

This is a dubious grey area. We've had a few instances of this kind of case. In one, a buyer bought a burgundy bridesmaid dress. The photos were unfiltered, but the buyer claimed that the color didn't match. She also claimed that a clasp-hook was missing. We replied by uploading photos of the manufacturer's color label and color swatch. While we won on the color, we lost on the missing clasp. We got the dress back in a timely manner and it was in the same condition with a nice note from the buyer. It turns out, the clasp was hidden but I didn't know that at the time. While disappointing, it wasn't the end of the world. We relisted it and eventually sold it to a happy customer. In another instance, we sold a bundle of three wedding gowns. They were clearly described with clear photos. We gave the buyer a great discount and shipped them all in one package. We had to buy extra postage (see chapter eight) since the standard flat rate label wasn't sufficient. Upon receiving the dresses, the buyer immediately opened a case and claimed that all three dresses were defective. The photos didn't show any damage. In this case, we were in the right and the buyer was simply unhappy with her purchase. So, what did we do? We refuted her claim with photos and accepted the return. That wasn't a misprint. We let Poshmark proceed with the return. If you're in this situation, you may do something different. For us, it was so clear that she was unhappy with her purchase, and although her claim was baseless, we decided to let her return them. All three dresses were returned in the same condition, and we re-listed them. In this instance, it wasn't worth forcing a sour grapes customer to accept a purchase even though we were clearly in the right. As for the extra postage we paid, Poshmark refunded that to us. Incidentally, this same customer came back a year or two later and bundled over 20 dresses and offered us a five-figure offer. To date, it was the highest offer we've gotten on Poshmark. What did we do? We declined. That's not a misprint either. I'll explain why. First, while the offer was five-figures, the offer was still too low. Second, we weren't selling these under a wholesale account so the shipping alone would have been a logistical nightmare. After we declined, she asked if we could cut a deal to sell her the dresses directly. She had apparently forgotten that she had previously purchased three dresses from us and returned them as an "unsatisfied customer." I bit my tongue or rather suppressed my fingers from typing any snarky comments, and politely declined. I did remind her, diplomatically and with no snark, that she was a previous unsatisfied customer and recommended she find a wholesaler. I always think it's better to be respectful since you never know who you'll do business with, in the future. By the same token, you have every right to decline an offer from someone who disrespects you or your business. Every now and then she still puts items into her still massive bundle.

Items over $500

As covered in chapter eight, items that sell for $500 or more fall into a separate set of procedures. Since those items are sent to Poshmark first and inspected by them before being dispatched to the customer, if a buyer opens a case, that is handled exclusively between Poshmark and buyer. We've had two instances of this with one being decided in our favor and the other being decided in the customer's. In the latter, we mistakenly labeled a wedding gown as white when it was ivory, and she had a legitimate cause to return it. Generally, items that were authenticated by Poshmark puts a higher burden on the buyer to make a convincing case for a return.

If you're notified that a case has been opened, don't panic. Take a deep breath and review the claim, along with any accompanying photos and statements. If the buyer doesn't provide photos, request them so that you can see the exact problem. You can also provide photos and statements of your own. As covered earlier, I recommend taking photos of an item before you pack it in case you need evidence. Be polite, patient, and pleasant in handling the situation. As you've seen from our examples, we've had the full gambit of situations from cases decided in our favor to returns that were abandoned (and thus closed) to cases that were decided against us; sometimes fairly and other times, not so (at least in my opinion). Don't let this scare you from selling on Poshmark. If you are upfront about what you're selling and take the time and care to thoroughly answer questions and ship packages in a timely manner, most of your transactions will be fine. However, it's important to know that these things can and do happen, especially as you grow your business. If necessary, review chapter 10. Remember, all sales are final means you have a higher responsibility as a seller.

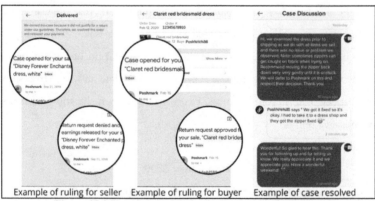

Example of ruling for seller   Example of ruling for buyer   Example of case resolved

Figure 17.3 Examples of different Poshmark decisions.

Oops

Now, I turn to my least favorite part of the book. The following are noteworthy mistakes we've made as a Poshmark seller.

Oops: Wrong label

Imagine, you've sold two or more items in a row over a weekend. You're on a roll. The first sale is a blue bridesmaid dress. You ship it out, then, a second sale comes in for a blue bridesmaid dress that looks identical to the first. You accidentally print out the first label and ship out the dress to the same customer you shipped the first dress to! I made this discovery when the second dress wouldn't update its shipping status in Poshmark. In this case, we had the USPS receipt with the tracking numbers. I compared them and noticed we accidentally used the wrong label.

Solution: What did I do? Panic. What did I do after that? I emailed Poshmark to see if they had procedures for correcting this. Next, I let the buyer know that I accidentally sent her package to the wrong address but that we would correct this. It's important to own up to your mistakes and let your customers know, especially if they may not get the package in a timely manner. Third, I apprised the person who would be receiving the package of the situation as well. This last party was the first to respond. Since it was a day or two later, she informed us she had just received it and kindly offered to help in any way she could. The second message was from the buyer who said it was no problem and appreciated the update. Poshmark responded third, letting us know they have procedures for this. However, being a very impatient person, I didn't wait for Poshmark's response. I asked the person who got the dress for a big favor. I offered to email her the correct shipping label and asked if she would mind dropping it off at USPS. I also communicated with the buyer to make sure she was ok with me providing the correct shipping label to the accidental recipient.

Since the mistaken recipient was also a Poshmark seller, she said it would be no problem since USPS regularly picks up packages from her. We sent her the label and the package was shipped the next day. I updated Poshmark to let them know that we corrected it ourselves. By then, the package was en route to the right customer and the tracking activated in the interim. The correct customer received it only a day later than expected and gave us a four-star rating. As a thanks to all, we sent Starbucks gift cards to both parties. This story should serve as a reminder to always double check your labels to ensure that your order numbers and buyer usernames match.

Oops: Wrong label, right item, right address

Ok, so here's a doozy for you which you probably won't ever run into but for completeness, I'll include this story even at the risk of further embarrassment. Imagine you sell an item. You go to pack it but can't find it. You search everywhere but it's nowhere to be found. This happened to us about two years ago. We closed a sale, and I called my dad. He couldn't find the dress and assumed he sold it in store, despite the listing having a check mark. I ended up cancelling the sale, which you can do through the app. When that happens, the buyer is refunded their money and you get an email telling you not to ship it. Five minutes later, my dad called to tell me he found the dress.

Ughhhh!

I let the buyer know, relisted it, and offered a discount for her troubles. She accepted and voila! Sale. However, my dad ended up printing out the label from the first, now cancelled sale. It had the right address, the right item, but the wrong tracking number. Again, I noticed this when the status didn't change from sold to shipped. After comparing tracking numbers, I discovered he used the wrong label.

Solution: I simply let Poshmark know and asked them to switch to the first tracking number so it could update. We let the customer know (this was not our finest hour) and sent her a small gift. It ended up fine and the customer was very happy. She got a great discount, and a gift, all because of our screw up. In the end, it was worth it. This customer was serving in the military, and we were happy to give her the red-carpet treatment. She left us an enthusiastic five-star review. Out of this mishap, we got a happy customer plus a memorable story for this chapter.

Remember, mistakes can happen even if you're careful. Also, threaded email chains suck.

No one's fault

As mentioned, in 2020 and 2021, the US Postal Service experienced unprecedented challenges in getting shipments delivered on time. I reiterate my admonition from chapter eight. Do not promise delivery dates.

During our first two years on the platform, almost all of our orders arrived to customers within two-to-three days, sometimes even within one. However, by late 2020 and into 2021, many shipments would take a day or two longer. We even had extreme situations, in which shipments took two-to-three weeks to arrive.

In October 2020, we sold a dress to a customer in Florida. We shipped and confirmed the same day and as usual, the tracking status changed to show it was in transit. However, one week went by, then two, then three, and the shipment was still in transit. We notified the customer and Poshmark and continued to monitor the situation via the tracking info. Finally, by December, the update showed it was "out for delivery." Then, nothing. The tracking never confirmed a delivery and another two weeks went by. Almost two months passed, and the package was off the radar. Poshmark ended up cancelling the transaction and reimbursing both parties. This was a situation of a lost shipment due to no one's fault and a crappy situation with the USPS.

In late December 2021, we sold a high-end wedding dress. Because it was over $500, it had to go to Poshmark first for authentication. We sent it out immediately and it arrived at Poshmark on time, a few days later. The dress, along with other items, sat there for over two weeks. In the interim, I contacted Poshmark several times and was informed that no one could be at the center at that time. I don't know for sure, but it was most likely due to a pandemic-related issue. Regardless, they informed me that authentications were delayed. It wasn't completed until Monday, January 3rd, 2022! In this situation, it was no one's fault. It was simply one of those once in a blue moon, worldwide pandemic situations. The only thing I could do was keep the buyer informed, which I did. Thankfully she was very understanding and appreciated the updates.

As of the writing of this chapter, things are mostly back to normal with two-to-three day delivery times. Knocking on wood, I hope as you begin your Poshmark journey that these stories become nothing more than historical anecdotes.

However, I can't tell the future. This is why it's important to realize that issues out of your control do happen. The best thing to do is communicate with your customer, and if necessary, loop in Poshmark. Use the tracking info to stay up to date and most of all, don't promise delivery dates!

One-star ratings

Currently, on Poshmark we have a 4.9 average rating, made up of 263 ratings, out of 350+ sales.

First, when it comes to ratings and reviews, don't push. If you do your job, they will come naturally. I hate it when I buy products and I get follow-up emails, asking for reviews. People who love your product and want to tell the world about it will do so. Others won't leave a review. That's ok too. You've made your sale and the money is in your account. Whether you get a review and rating is up to the buyer.

Out of the star ratings, I'm pleased to say that the majority are 5-star ratings. That's as high as you can get. Full disclosure: as of the writing of this chapter, we have 253 five-star, 9 four-star, 2 three-star, 1 two-star, and 2 one-star ratings. The rest as you can guess are closed sales with no ratings or reviews.

Let me give you my perspective on ratings and why you shouldn't panic about getting a one-star or two-star rating if it happens.

If you do your job, meaning you're accurate about your listings and you ship in a timely manner, you will do well on Poshmark. The majority of your customers will be happy, and you'll make money. If there's a problem, there are channels to resolve it as explored above and even then, many of those customers will leave enthusiastic reviews and ratings. Poshmark, for the most part, attracts great customers who want to love what they buy. This is why I say that "all sales final" puts a higher degree of responsibility on sellers.

Regardless, if you sell long enough, you will probably get at least one one-star rating. I would go so far as to say that if you become a five, six, or seven figure seller, you will get at least a few one and two star reviews. It's a "when" rather than "if" question and inevitable, given the law of averages. The first time we got a one-star rating was early on in our Poshmark journey. We had around a dozen sales under our belt with a solid five-star average rating. Then, we sold a brand name coat at a good discount. The buyer received it, the three-day inspection window passed, the sale closed, and we never heard anything. About two weeks later, we received a one-star rating along with a scathing comment insinuating the coat was a "knock-off." I assure you it wasn't. My dad's shop was a licensed carrier of this brand from years ago, and we had one leftover coat in mint condition. It had all the tags and was a beautiful, hard to find item. We also sold it at a nice discount for the buyer. So, when this customer left a one-star review, it stung. When I read the comment, I was incensed. It could have been grounds for a product defamation lawsuit. I normally don't respond to reviews for reasons I'll discuss shortly, but this was over the line. I tagged the buyer in the comments, acknowledging that she was not happy with the purchase but sternly and politely refuted her accusation. I called her out on it and advised her to file a complaint with Poshmark. She never replied.

Another time, we sold a dress at full price and about a week after the return window passed, got a one-star rating without any comment. While disappointing, I didn't pursue it.

Poshmark has a section on seller profiles called "love notes." If a customer leaves a four- or five-star review along with comments, it will display them to the public. At this time, it does not display negative comments attached to one or two-star reviews, hence the name "love notes." So, don't panic if you get a bad review or rating. If you do your job, these should be an outlier, not a common occurrence.

You may be surprised to read this, but I wouldn't mind if Poshmark decided to make all comments visible in the "love notes" section, whether attached to five-star or one-star ratings. And yes, that would require a re-branding of "love notes." If you're upfront about what you're selling, provide good service, and sell with integrity, your business will not falter because of a bad review or rating. As you close more sales, the law of averages will provide a fair and accurate picture of you as a seller.

Thus, when it comes to ratings and reviews, I generally don't respond or follow-up. You may take a different approach, but I feel that a review and rating is the opinion of a buyer. Aside from over-the-top comments, the only time I respond is if there's a question or comment that merits doing something to make the sale an even better experience. In one case, we got a perfect five-star rating and a glowing review. However, in the review, the buyer noted a bead was missing while acknowledging that since the dress came with extra beads, she could easily fix it. While it was a great review, I wanted to do something more, so I sent her a Starbucks gift card. She later posted in our bundle chat that the gesture was above and beyond her expectations. Sometimes, it's worth it to go the extra mile to make a great experience even better.

Those exceptions aside, I generally don't follow-up on reviews. When I was in law school, a trial professor once told our class that you don't thank the judge for sustaining your objection or overruling one from the other side. It's their job and crosses a line to thank them for doing it. I treat reviews and ratings the same way. Unless it's an issue or question that needs to be addressed, it's best to let the person's rating and review stand alone. Thanking them can feel a bit invasive. Again, this is just me. Some sellers go out of their way to thank buyers for reviews. You may be inclined to do so and that's fine.

As you build your Poshmark business, know that mistakes sometimes happen. Platforms aren't perfect. People aren't perfect. Do the best you can and when problems arise, stay calm, work through it, and be polite, patient, and pleasant. I'm going to reiterate my statement from the start of this chapter. Don't let these scenarios scare you. We've had our fair share of mishaps, bad reviews, and ratings, and we're still here, surviving and thriving. Finally, learn from these situations. Take each bump in the road as an opportunity to improve.

Too often, I see business books overlook the bad and overplay the good. I don't want to give you a lopsided picture. Rather, I want you to learn from my mistakes so you can avoid or minimize them. This is why I included this chapter. It's worth it for me to risk a little embarrassment so you can achieve greater success.

❧ BEST PRACTICE TIPS:
- o Triple check orders to make sure labels match items, order numbers, and buyer usernames.
- o The packing slips feature covered in chapter 15 can provide an extra spot check for shipments.
- o If you take it upon yourself to correct a situation, notify all parties involved. Otherwise, contact Poshmark support for guidance.

🌑 **EXERCISE:** Check out the "love notes" within the profiles of different Poshmark sellers. If you've sold items and are receiving reviews and ratings, look at your own. See where you can improve, get an idea of benchmarks and milestones to achieve, including faster shipping times to increase your ratings average.

PART III

18 LEVELING UP YOUR BUSINESS

While this book primarily focuses on getting started on Poshmark, I thought you might be interested to see where we are now, how we've grown the business, and how we've given back.

Online to in-person

You might be surprised to learn that Poshmark has helped our in-person retail business. Due to our increased presence on the web, we've attracted customers from all over the country, including ones from our backyard who didn't know about us before. We're often asked where we're located and have gained new customers from Maryland and neighboring states who have visited in person. Through these interactions, we've closed sales and cultivated relationships. As I write this chapter, we recently had a customer from Maryland who had been searching for a rare wedding gown for months. As it happened, we had this specific dress listed on Poshmark for over a year. It's an older style, and hard to come by, but this was the only one she wanted for her special day. She saw the listing from our closet and messaged us in a bundle, asking about size. Since a wedding gown is a big purchase, not to mention an important part of a big life event, she wanted to make sure it would fit. When she discovered we're in the same state, she asked if she could come in person to try it on. She booked an appointment, came in, tried on the dress and it was indeed a perfect fit. She not only ended up buying it but her mom who accompanied her ended up buying a dress for the wedding. As much as I started our journey looking for an ecommerce solution, I never imagined that it would increase in-person sales and customers. This has been one of the unexpected ancillary benefits of being on Poshmark.

Online to less in-person

It's a given that the pandemic has forever changed every aspect of our lives and in ways we can't fully comprehend yet. In the world of retail, bankruptcy filings of famous department stores dominated the business headlines throughout 2020 and 2021. However, these articles overlooked small retail businesses like my dad's that were devastated by the pandemic. In late 2020, many states mandated non-essential business closure orders, hampering their ability to stay afloat. As I write this chapter, our state, along with many others are moving back to some semblance of normalcy. Yet, there's a lot of doubt and uncertainty over the future of in-person retail. Meanwhile, online vendors like Amazon have seen unprecedented growth; a change that's likely here to stay.

Poshmark was one of the few lifelines we had during these past few years to keep the business going. Today, many are still understandably hesitant to venture into a store if they don't have to. In 2016, taking the business online was borne out of needing to stay competitive. Today, it's a matter of survival in a post-pandemic world that looks very different than anything we've experienced before.

Wholesale buying and Boutique selling

If you plan to grow your Poshmark business, you may want to explore the world of wholesale. Wholesale means buying items in bulk at a lower cost per unit. As a reminder, labelling your items as "boutique" simply means you've purchased directly from a wholesaler as opposed to a store. To sell items using the "boutique" label, go into "My Sellers Tools" and complete a short certification questionnaire to access this feature.

The distinction between listing an item as "boutique" and "new with tags" is minor as both are technically the same condition: new (not used or worn) items with the original tags. The difference is more for sellers than buyers. Most buyers won't care whether a listing is categorized as "boutique" or "new with tags" and many won't know what "boutique" means. As a result, we often get questions about whether an item is new or used.

Wholesale shopping has traditionally been a strictly business-to-business (B2B) channel for retail stores like my dad's. In the past, small retail businesses used agents and brokers to connect with suppliers and wholesalers. This required a lot of time, expense, and relationship building. Unless you run a retail business, it's not something most people would want or need to get into.

Most Poshmark sellers list used clothes from their closets. Others buy attractive used items from thrift stores or new items from retail stores that are marked down (think "Black Friday" or "going out of business" sales), and list them at a markup. For the former, the incentive is to clear out space while making some dollars on something old ("salvage value"). For the latter, it's to make a profit through "retail arbitrage."

To illustrate, suppose you go to your local big box store and find a pair of jeans that normally retail at $40. You buy them on sale for $20 and sell them on Poshmark for $35. You've cleared a nice profit based on what you paid for them. Now, suppose you want to keep selling the same jeans because they're popular and move quickly. You go back to the same store and want to buy 10 more pairs but find only three left or worse, the sale has ended, and the price is now back to $40.

With a business like my dad's, he has the same goal as a retail arbitrager: buy low, sell high. However, a brick-and-mortar store can't sustain itself with one-off items. Also, while buying individual items on sale can be fun, it's time consuming and difficult to scale. That's where wholesale purchasing comes in.

Let's go back to the designer jeans example. Suppose a wholesaler will sell you the same jeans, brand new and right off the factory line, for $10 apiece. You could sell for $35 or more and clear a profit that's even greater than if you bought it on sale at the big box store. The catch is that to get the $10 per jean price, you need to buy 100 pairs, which would cost $1000. That's wholesale buying in a nutshell. It's buying in bulk like when you go to Costco to get a gigantic two-pack of flour, or five boxes of pasta. The individual unit cost is lower, but you must buy a larger quantity.

On Poshmark, sellers can now access wholesale accounts and buy in bulk, whether it's sweaters, dresses, socks, or shoes. As of the writing of this chapter, you must have a minimum of ten sales and a 4.5 average rating or higher to access wholesalers on Poshmark. Once you meet the minimum threshold, you can access and shop from wholesale sellers.

For the more adventurous, there are online platforms like Alibaba that allow retailers to source products directly from suppliers in different countries, at lower unit costs.

Since my dad is already in the retail business, he's been plugged into buying wholesale his entire business life. For most of you starting out, you won't touch wholesale buying until and unless you've achieved a lot of sales and are ready (and desire) to scale your business. Thus, I recommend start out with clearing your closet or doing retail arbitrage: buying and listing items you find at thrift stores or on sale. You may find that satisfying enough. Many sellers have built up successful side and even full-time businesses just doing that. Incidentally, Poshmark has a program for those who want to sell wholesale. There's a separate application process with specific requirements to become a wholesaler on the platform. Once approved, you will be assigned a wholly separate account for wholesale selling. Since this book is mostly focused on individual selling, I'll leave it at that.

Before we leave this part of the chapter, here's quick refresher and glossary:

- **Boutique:** you're selling items that you've purchased wholesale or directly from a supplier (as opposed to bought off the rack, in which case they're "new with tags").
- **Wholesale buying:** you're buying items in bulk at a lower cost per unit but with a minimum purchase quantity.
- **Wholesale selling:** you're selling items in bulk at a lower cost per unit with a minimum purchase quantity.

Figure 18.1 Boutique certification.

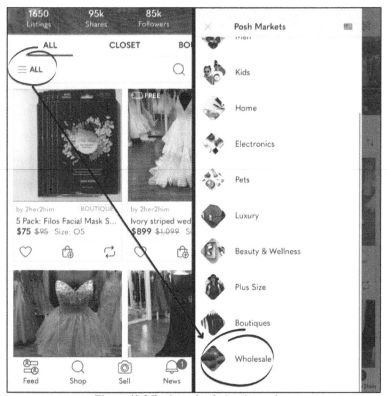

Figure 18.2 Poshmark wholesale market.

Giving back

When I started helping my dad with his online business six years ago, I never expected it to be more than finding a solution to a problem. That's exactly how I looked at it. He needed a way to be more current and competitive and we spent over two years experimenting with different platforms towards achieving that goal. When we got on Poshmark, and started gaining traction, I was thrilled but never saw it as more than a business strategy, plain and simple. That all changed in spring 2019.

A woman placed a bid on a prom dress that we had listed for sale. The bid wasn't very high and at first, we didn't consider it a "serious" offer based on the ZOA. The bid would barely cover the cost of the dress, even at wholesale cost. Initially, we counter-offered and soon after, the person posted a question. As I covered earlier, one of my pet peeves is when someone asks about pricing offers. However, this comment was different. She asked if there was any flexibility in the price, explaining that she sponsors young teens who otherwise can't afford to go to their proms. As part of this, she helps young women with hair and makeup, and buys their dresses.

I talked it over with my dad and we were both touched by her story and mission. My dad regularly donates dresses in his local area, supporting similar causes. However, this was the first time we came across a similar need on Poshmark. We decided to make an exception and asked her to re-submit her bid, which we accepted. We shipped out the dress and when she received it the following week, she thanked us, letting us know that she would post photos on social media.

This sale did not make us much money, but it felt great to help these two people we would probably never meet. I know next to nothing about clothes, and I always saw my dad's business as supply and demand. But here was someone supporting a young person so she would get to experience an important milestone. Best of all, this person was well beyond our state borders. Taking my dad's business online has been a joy and a pathway to achieve scale and success. But it's also allowed us to make a difference, if in a small way. I now have a better understanding of why my dad loves what he does. If you start selling on Poshmark and build a business, my hope is that you'll have an opportunity, and the means to occasionally forgo a profit to bring some joy and happiness into someone's life.

More recently, we pivoted my dad's business in 2020 and 2021 to compensate for the loss of in-store revenue since proms were mostly cancelled and weddings postponed. During this time, my dad shifted his resources and talents to produce personal protective equipment (PPE), including masks, which he donated to the state of Maryland to give to frontline workers and those in need. Throughout 2020 and the first half of 2021, we included a free mask with each purchase on Poshmark. It was a small way to show our love and thanks to our many customers.

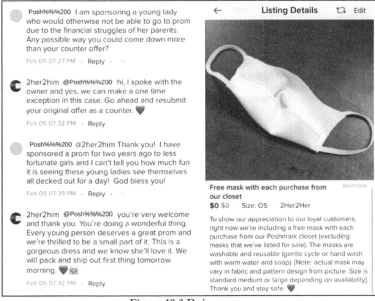

Figure 18.3 Doing more.

Finally, one recent upgrade that I applaud, which distinguishes Poshmark from many other platforms is that buyers can now purchase items, listed over a certain amount, with an installment plan. Poshmark has partnered with "Affirm" (symbol: AFRM), which allows buyers to choose three, six, or 12-month installments. This is a game changer for those who want to buy higher end or more expensive items but cannot afford a one-time lump payment. When we started listing expensive wedding gowns and name-brand dresses, we were often asked about installment plans but that was not an option in 2018. It was either an all or nothing transaction with negotiating in between. Today, buyers can choose to split up payments to make larger purchases viable.

Figure 18.4 Installment option through Affirm.

The future

Poshmark continues to expand its breadth and reach. With the current climate, more people are buying and selling online; a trend that will likely continue for years to come.

I don't have a crystal ball but if I had to make a prediction, it's that Poshmark will become a global marketplace for many types of goods. Beyond the US, the platform is available in Canada and recently expanded into Australia and India. Beyond clothes, Poshmark has since launched a separate category called "home goods," allowing people to buy and sell items such as bedspreads, office supplies, and even wall art. Poshmark has also expanded to pet supplies and in late 2021, electronics, both high growth areas.

We're also seeing an evolution in the way sellers can market their items. "Ecommerce 1.0" as I call it, is the traditional model of marketing with photos and copy, and external promotion on social media. Poshmark evolved this into 2.0 with a built-in community of sellers and buyers, and by introducing video into the mix. In doing so, Poshmark created an entry point for sellers that lack robust social media presences while enabling popular influencers to leverage their large audiences through integrations with Facebook, Instagram, Twitter, and more recently Snapchat. I believe 3.0 is around the corner. With the rise of metaverse technologies, including augmented and virtual reality capabilities, we will see interesting and exciting applications for clothing. Virtual fitting rooms, virtual assistants, and artificial intelligence may very well make age-old conundrums like sizing uncertainty a thing of the past.

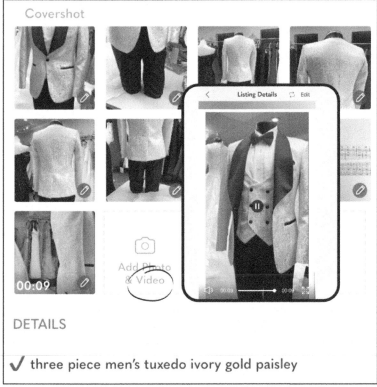

Figure 18.5 Video took ecommerce to 2.0. What's next?

🔹 **BEST PRACTICE TIPS:**
   o   Video listings: shoot in portrait ("tall") mode showcasing a 360-degree view of the item.
   o   Optional: edit videos in apps like iMovie and add music and / or voiceover narration.

❧ **EXERCISE:** Go back to your exercise from chapter one. Now, think ahead to a future time, be it one year, two years, or more and write out your Poshmark goal(s) for the distant future.

_____

_____

_____

_____

_____

19 OTHER PLATFORMS AND LARGER THEMES

In chapter one, I talked about our journey with ecommerce, starting out with Amazon FBA, eBay, and Shopify. In this chapter, I'll cover the landscape more in detail. The purpose of this chapter isn't to slam or denigrate any of these platforms but to give you our full story and to demonstrate that ecommerce solutions aren't one-size fits all. Each platform has its plusses and minuses, and you may find greater success with them than we did. Instead, I want to draw out some larger themes that will give you a basis from which to approach ecommerce selling so you can be successful no matter where you choose to sell.

eBay

Sometime in 2008, my dad first came up with the idea of selling online. This wasn't driven by need but more by curiosity. He mentioned eBay, which has been around for a while. My familiarity with it was as a broader marketplace where people would sell old items for auction. It was the "my trash is someone else's treasure" platform. Even as early as 2008, eBay had grown into a significant marketplace, right up there with Amazon. What I didn't know was that at the time, eBay had a small business and merchant section, in which sellers who had established businesses could open shop and run a virtual store. It was a paid subscription, costing around $29 a month. We set up shop, and the listing process was cumbersome. The most memorable part of that experience were the fees, both upfront and hidden. In addition to the monthly subscription, there were fees for listing, for adding pictures (beyond the standard one or two), and fees for sales. While most of these were in the cents range, it wasn't entirely clear how much they would eat into our bottom line.

The next big hurdle was shooting and uploading photos. At the time, smartphones were in their infancy so that wasn't really an option as neither of us had one. We did however have a digital camera that stored photos onto a minidisk. We took photos of several items, and as mentioned, the eBay merchant account only allowed a set number. To save costs, I found a service that enabled you to link your eBay account to a separate online photo album. Next, we wanted to drive sales by offering free return shipping as that was and still is, a big driver for many who buy online. To facilitate this, we had to go to the Post Office and open a special account for return labels that would be billed to us. This was a bigger hassle than the last sentence captures. At the time, no one had made this request before at our USPS location. Someone had to dust off a binder with the correct procedures. After an hour or two, we set up an account; filling out a bunch of forms and got a stack of return labels.

We opened up shop to the sound of crickets. Mostly, we got a few inquiries but no sales. Further, there was a lot of confusion as we were not selling by auction but using a "buy it now" default for merchant accounts. We lasted about three or four months before closing our virtual shop. We still have a stack of those return labels in a drawer somewhere. Today, eBay has evolved and there are many sellers, including small businesses that use it as a robust ecommerce channel. I later returned to eBay when I had the small fledging skincare line that I briefly mentioned at the beginning of the book. We actually sold a skin moisturizer on eBay at full price. So, while I can say I've sold something on eBay, I'm hardly a success story with it. That said, eBay really kicked off the ecommerce revolution and continues to be a go-to platform for many who sell online.

Amazon FBA

As I discussed earlier, ecommerce became more prominent on our radar in 2016. Up until then, in-store retail still had a customer base that was very distinct from people who shopped online. However, this was starting to change rapidly, particularly with clothing. My dad noticed a growing number of customers who would come in to browse, get fitted, snap photos, and leave. We would later find out that people were using in-store visits for measurements only to buy online, either directly from a retailer or from Amazon, which was increasingly getting a foothold in the clothing sphere. Coincidentally, this was also the period, in which Facebook (now Meta) was chock full of ads that microtargeted users. Many consider it the "golden age" of online advertising as you could run ads for pennies with huge results. Since I was doing a lot of research on Amazon, I saw ads for courses, webinars, books, and services touting "how to sell on Amazon" secrets. I'm sure I saw a few ads from Amazon itself on there. I attended a couple of free webinars and learned that there were a growing number of intrepid entrepreneurs setting up virtual retail shops through Amazon and doing everything from retail arbitrage to drop shopping; a tactic in which a seller fulfills an order by having a third-party supplier ship directly to the customer. The most intriguing thing I learned was that Amazon had a Fulfilled by Amazon (FBA) program, a relatively new initiative at the time, in which sellers could open merchant accounts, and ship products directly to Amazon for storage and fulfillment. There were several advantages to this model. First, sellers could leverage Amazon's massive supply chain fulfillment processes, including access to its nationwide storage centers and sophisticated online inventory management systems. Second, and most appealing, merchants could tap into Amazon Prime, a subscription service in which items can be ordered from Amazon with no shipping cost. I gave my dad a brief presentation and he was both intrigued and awed that this was even a thing. We decided to give it a try. As with eBay's business program, Amazon had a subscription for its business accounts costing around $39.95 per month. We set up our account and what I remember most were the hoops we had to jump through to set up a clothing store online. I'll list some of the highlights below.

If you want to sell certain product categories on Amazon FBA, you must apply for approval. This includes clothing. Fortunately, my dad has a business license as a clothing merchant, which got him immediate approval. This hoop was the easiest for us to jump through but may prove tricky for those of who are new to selling.

Navigating the listing process proved to be the most painful and cumbersome with FBA. First, the system was hardly intuitive. I'm pretty good at figuring out most systems, having grown up with an Atari 2600, later graduating to DOS, Windows, Mac, and today, I'm fairly adept at using my iPhone, Macbook, and Surface. But I developed a serious case of wrinkled brow trying to create listings on Amazon. The menus, categories, and options were overwhelming: it was a bear just to type in information and format it properly. Pictures were another challenge. New merchants must use photos with all white backgrounds using mannequins and no models. First, we tried asking our suppliers, many of whom provided photos for my dad's website and in-store catalog, to see if they could send us these kinds of photos. Somehow "sure, no problem" changed within the English language because what seemed like an easy ask resulted in one supplier sending us photos that were the same as before on a colored background, another sending us photos with models, and another that had taken their original photos and badly whitened out the background through poor photoshopping. At the time I was renting an office and my downstairs neighbor happened to be a media company with a photo studio. The head of the media company was nice enough to loan me the space in the evenings after everyone went home, and we hired a photographer to do a photoshoot. By now, we were into early 2017, approximately five months after we opened our FBA account. After spending lots of time and money, we got usable photos but there was one more major hurdle. Products listed on FBA had to have a specific barcode. The problem was a lot of the clothes we sold didn't have barcodes or had ones that weren't compatible with FBA. This is where I learned that the clothing industry isn't consistent in labeling standards. Just as a size small from one brand doesn't equate to a small from another, labels don't always come with barcodes. So, we had to buy barcodes. Where do you buy barcodes? There are lots of places, but I ended up buying a thousand or so from eBay! If you're getting tired, we're not done yet. Once we jumped through all the listing hoops, we had to send the clothes to Amazon's FBA warehouse. This meant we had to pay for shipping and wait for delivery and processing before the listings could go live. After all of that, we managed to get about a dozen listings up on FBA after six months of work. Keep in mind, I only work with my dad once or twice a week so that partly explains why it took so long. But even if I had worked with him every day, a FBA listing would take a good two or three weeks to go live. I later tried FBA with the aforementioned skin cleanser, and that's about how long it took to get our product listed for sale.

Now, the results. We ended up selling around six or seven items, including a couple of dresses and a raincoat. We didn't do any additional advertising either. This was purely the result of being on Amazon's ecosystem, which was a huge positive. In addition, Amazon took care of fulfilling and shipping the orders. We would get notification emails informing us that an item had been ordered and shipped, which meant we didn't have to do anything else on our part. That was another huge upside to selling on FBA.

The downside, however, was threefold. First, the amount of time required to get new listings up meant we couldn't do this quickly or easily. At the pace we were moving, we could only do a few items at a time. Second, Amazon, like eBay, has a lot of ancillary fees. There are fees for shipping products to Amazon, fees for sales, and monthly long-term storage fees if the products don't move quickly. By far though, the biggest pain point was Amazon's "no questions asked" return policy. As a result, the excitement for seller notification emails was mostly short lived as we would receive "buyer has returned item" emails on many of these purchases a few weeks later. Of the seven or so items we sold, only about three closed, meaning the buyer kept the item past the return window. The rest we got shipped directly to us, as you can guess, on our dime. We decided to close our Amazon FBA store in late 2017 and had the rest of our inventory sent back to us (again, on our dime) just before the long-term storage fees kicked in.

Shopify

Around the same time that we were navigating the ins and outs of FBA, I gave a speech at Johns Hopkins Business School, my business school alma mater. Afterward, I met an MBA student who was about to graduate and was deciding between taking a job in finance or starting a business selling her own cosmetics line. I was intrigued and encouraged her to stay in touch. A year or two later, I found out she opened an online store, selling her own nail lacquer line. She sourced everything from the formula to her own uniquely designed bottles and boxes, all from different manufacturers across the US and as far abroad as Italy. She was also doing quite well, leveraging social media, and building up a significant following. I invited her to talk about her business on my podcast, and we spoke about her entrepreneurial journey. Afterward, we talked about ecommerce, and she told me that she had originally hired a web designer but had a bad experience outsourcing it and had recently migrated her shop to Shopify. She customized her store's website and that's when business took off. I investigated Shopify as we were experiencing our hurdles with FBA. We decided to try Shopify and set up a merchant account. As with eBay and FBA, this required a monthly subscription fee. We opted for an expensive plan costing around $250 a month. Unlike eBay and Amazon, Shopify had a great feature, which I hope becomes more common across all platforms. The pro plans included subaccounts that you could allocate to employees to do limited tasks like create listings without giving them access to the more sensitive parts, including banking and gross revenue information. Shopify also had an easier listing process than either Amazon or eBay save for one major shortfall. With clothing, you often have one piece with several sizes. A dress may come in small, medium, large, or numeric sizes such as 2, 4, 6, 8, 10, 12, etc. While this sounds like a straightforward task, it was extremely cumbersome on Shopify. There was no easy way, at least in 2018, to list size variations. I had to research work arounds that required plugins and html coding. Moreover, as I was becoming more immersed in ecommerce, I realized how much I wanted a mobile option. While ubiquitous today, I was part of the generation that was tethered to the desktop. However, since a lot of the collaboration I do with my dad is remote, having to wait until I could get in front of a desktop or laptop proved to be a headache. While Shopify did have a mobile app, back then, the functionality was limited at best. We lasted about six months with a Shopify store without closing a single sale. While the set up was easier than FBA or eBay, generating sales required investing a lot of resources and energy into marketing our website through social and traditional media. We simply didn't have the bandwidth or budget to do that.

You know the rest from the start of this book. I found Poshmark by accident and most of this book has focused on how we generated sales and achieved scale on the platform. Again, the purpose of this chapter isn't to slam or criticize any of the other ecommerce solutions. They all come with their strengths and competitive advantages. However, for our purposes, none proved to be as ideal as Poshmark for a small clothing business.

The biggest and most refreshing change was Poshmark's mobile-centric platform. As I transitioned off Shopify and onto Poshmark, I realized how much I welcomed and needed an out-of-the-box mobile solution. I could name any number of reasons as to why I believe it's the better platform for selling clothes but the three biggest from our experiences are 1) its all in one mobile interface, 2) its social selling aspect with a built-in community of buyers, and 3) its simple fee structure that doesn't require a monthly subscription.

Over the past decade or so, many mobile selling platforms have popped out of the woodwork. In addition to Poshmark, today you have Mercari, Depop, OfferUp, thredUP, Curtsy, Vinted, Flyp, and Grailed, to name a few. There will probably be several more by the time you read this chapter. Some are specialized by clothing genre or age demographic, while others cater to high end or luxury labels, and still others are touted as broader selling apps. In addition, platforms like Facebook and Instagram have created their own virtual marketplaces, which are becoming this generations' garage or yard sale. We're seeing a shift away from desktop and web-based ecommerce platforms in favor of on-the-go mobile apps that enable easy set-up and immediate access to ready marketplaces. Moreover, many of these platforms are leveraging a growing consumer trend that prefers mission-driven or eco-friendly business models. Poshmark was built on a reuse, recycle, and resell ethos for individuals. Our success with it proves that it is a viable solution for small businesses that do not have a large social media presence.

Admittedly, I have not tried all of the newer platforms. My experience is limited to the OG platforms discussed at the beginning of this chapter and Poshmark. I also fully admit that my experience with FBA, eBay, and Shopify are stuck in the past. I have not kept up with their evolution nor their developments and advancements. The key point here is that ecommerce is no longer just a niche or elusive way of selling as there are many user-friendly options available now. Moreover, for large and small businesses, an ecommerce option is necessary for survival and future growth. As discussed in the introduction, throughout 2020 and into 2021, major brands invested millions into developing ecommerce channels to answer a rising demand for "click and go" shopping solutions during the pandemic. However, I would argue that this trend towards buying online has been ongoing for many years. Even as we exit out of the pandemic, ecommerce is here to stay and demand for online order options will only continue to increase. While this book is geared mostly towards Poshmark, the principles I have shared on branding, marketing, engagement, and customer service are tried and true ones that will serve you well no matter which platform you use. Poshmark has proven to be a great solution, offering many features that were ideal for us. However, we didn't generate our first sale until we learned a new language of ecommerce selling. For any small business that wants to make this leap, it not only requires time and effort but changing the way you approach selling. Sharing your competitors' listings, engaging in activities like Poshmark parties, negotiating, and marketing your line through photos and video all require rethinking the way we do business.

> ● **EXERCISE:** Check out some other platforms. Do some research and see what the pros and cons are of each. If you're feeling adventurous, open an account on one or two or more platforms and try them out. Compare and contrast your experience with selling on Poshmark.

20 WRAPPING UP POSHMARK

Over these 20 chapters, we've covered a lot of principles, tactics, and strategies to start a business or expand one through Poshmark. By now, you should have completed the exercises, set up your Poshmark store, branded it, created some listings, engaged within the community, whether individually or at parties, and hopefully, closed your first sales. At the very least, you should have some concrete goals in mind for starting your Poshmark business and where you want to take it. Keep at it, and remember, this is a long game that will increase in speed and momentum as you invest more time and energy into it.

Poshmark is continually evolving. During the writing of this book alone, the app has undergone several major changes, including a facelift, the addition of video, and more recently advanced features like bulk sharing and "My Shoppers." You can even create a QR code for your store. I wouldn't be surprised if by the time you read this chapter there will be several more. However, I wouldn't worry about the newest bell or whistle because when it comes down to it, whether you sell in person, on Poshmark, or elsewhere, I believe there are two fundamental principles that are necessary to be successful.

Be responsive

As a reminder, we didn't get immediate traction on Poshmark, and to this day, we still don't have a major social media presence or following to tap into. I treated it like a "list it and leave it" sales platform and nothing more. Poshmark is really about engaging within a community. It blends ecommerce with elements of social media. Being responsive means answering questions, going above and beyond with your photos and copy, and supporting your fellow Poshers. Don't just sit back and wait for things to happen. Responding and engaging is the cornerstone for building momentum that leads to sales and relationships with customers from all over the country and perhaps, one day, the world.

Be organized

Whether you list five items or 500, you must be organized with your inventory and your time. Many of you will start on Poshmark as a side hustle, which means you're balancing it with other responsibilities. You can be successful even if you only have a few minutes a day to spend on the app. To this day, we manage it as part of a larger business, and we've done so without having to break rules or build up a social media following. The key is knowing your schedule and carving out strategic pockets of time. Moreover, you can structure your Poshmark business so that it works within your schedule.

Final thoughts

We're still building our business and recently closed our 357th sale, not counting in-store sales that resulted from Poshmark connections. I have a confession to make. I wasn't sure I was ready to write this book. I originally wanted to pitch this to a publisher and had secured a literary agent in 2021. We worked on a book proposal, and she advocated for it, recognizing its need and market potential. As we moved into early 2022, two things happened. First, every major publisher rejected the proposal. Second, my agent left to join another agency and couldn't take any of her clients with her. I was back to square one. I had a parade of insecurities raining in my head. Here are a few:

- "If only we had six figure sales ..."
- "If only we had a million followers ..."
- "If only we had a bigger social media presence ..."

- "If only we had more media coverage …"

I had a bad case of what's often referred to as "imposter syndrome." It's easy to get stuck in your head and think you're not enough; to think that you must hit a bigger yard stick before "justifying" writing a book. But then, I thought back to our first sale in September 2018, when we sold a pair of blue jeans. We experienced so much frustration over the past few years, trying to find the right platform, and when we finally did, it was a lot of trial and error with no sales in the beginning. By the time we got that first sale, we were both elated and exhausted. No matter what you see or hear on social media or what any "guru" or "expert" will tell you, this is not easy. Selling anything is hard. If you sell one item, you've accomplished something significant. And this reminded me why I wrote this book in the first place. It wasn't to convince a publisher that this topic is worthy of a traditionally published book. The reason I wrote this is because we're at a critical inflection point. Small retail businesses, especially in the clothing sector cannot continue without an online presence. It's no longer a nice to have, it's necessary for survival.

Moreover, while I may not yet be at the six or seven-figure sales mark, I firmly believe this book and our experiences will give you the tools to help you achieve your goals and aspirations. Keep in mind, selling on Poshmark is not my main job, nor is it the exclusive channel for my dad's business. It's a significant pipeline that we continue to invest time and energy into. If you're looking for a book that has six or seven figures in it, there are others out there. We're still on that journey, growing and learning along the way. I just didn't feel it necessary to wait to pass on what we've learned just for a sexier title.

Today, we average anywhere from zero-to-five sales a week and I think it's important to keep that perspective. Sometimes, you have sales raining in, other times you don't. But overall, this has been a net positive for our business and a lifeline to navigate the past several years of uncertainty and turmoil. That's why we treat each sale, big or small, as if it were our first and as if it's for a thousand-dollar item. Your attitude and gratitude are important for giving each customer a great shopping experience and making it a worthwhile venture for you. My hope is that this book will get you to wherever it is you want to go and in as short a time frame as possible by learning from what we did right but also what we did wrong.

We are in unpredictable and unprecedented times. As we exit the pandemic, we face hyperinflation, international turmoil, supply chain bottlenecks, and a shifting consumer mindset. Online purchasing, contactless payments, social distancing, and negotiating price are no longer just convenient. They're part of a "new normal." The sooner you understand this, both as a consumer and a seller, the easier it will be for you to adapt, survive, and thrive. And while the small retail business outlook is uncertain, there is a glimmer of hope. According to Poshmark's 2020 Social Commerce Report, there are 60 million users in the US and Canada. To date, the platform has generated 100 million orders and over $2B in annual sales. Poshmark and platforms like it are creating new businesses, built on a fluid model. Poshmark sellers include single moms, college students, teachers and other working professionals, celebrities, social media influencers, retirees, and as covered in this book, brick-and-mortar retail businesses.[10]

Whatever your goals are, whether it's to clear out your closet for extra cash or launch a new business venture, you've taken a first big step by reading this book and opening your store. Now it's time for you to see where this adventure will take you. Remember, having the right platform is important but how well you do is determined by your time, energy, and care. The door is wide open for you, and I wish you much prosperity and success.

APPENDICES

APPENDIX 1: EXERCISES

Chapter 1

● **EXERCISE:** In one or two sentences, write out your goal(s) for selling online. Specify why you want to sell clothes online. Are you doing this to clear out your closet or develop a business or side hustle? Where do you see your business or venture in six months or one year.

_____

_____

_____

_____

_____

Chapter 2

● **EXERCISE:** Dig into Poshmark: feel free to research articles like I did (good and bad, pros and cons) and read through Poshmark's website. Check out the fee structure. Remember, Poshmark doesn't charge a setup or listing fee and takes its commission post-sales. Next, download the Poshmark app and set up your account. Spend time on branding your store. (Estimated time: 10 minutes):

   o   Download the app and set up your store.
   o   Give it a name and handle (Poshmark user ID): come up with something that's easy such as your initials, a play on your name or, if you're a business, a username that matches your brand.
   o   Fill in some basic info.
   o   Upload a header and bio photo.

If you're feeling adventurous, list your first item. We'll go over the process in more detail in the next chapters so you can also wait if you're not quite ready for that.

Chapter 3

● **EXERCISE:** Find a space within your home or storefront to create listings. You don't need a professional studio. A nice corner of your home will do fine. Use that space to create consistent looking photos. Practice taking photos of multiple angles. Use a mannequin or ask a friend to be your model. Experiment and adjust lighting conditions as needed. You don't need fancy equipment. Often, a lamp or open window with daylight exposure will do just fine. If you build up your business and decide to invest more time, energy, and money, you can always upgrade your lighting and staging equipment later.

Chapter 4

● **EXERCISE:** Practice creating a listing video. Try getting it all in one shot, within 15 seconds, doing a 360 walk around your garment. Experiment with lighting, positioning, and your method.

- **BONUS EXERCISE:** Spruce up your video with music and / or voiceover. Come up with your own marketing style. Voiceover can be anything from explaining conditions, sizing, and colors to painting a picture of what occasion a particular listing might be great for.

Chapter 5

- **EXERCISE:** As you list your items, consider the condition, age, and profit margin or salvage value. If you're new to this, write it out. This will eventually become second nature.

Item	
• Original price	
• Age and Condition	
• Profit margin or salvage value	

Chapter 6

- **EXERCISE:** Pop Quiz. If someone posts a message asking you to contact them directly by email or phone to buy the item you've listed, you:

A. Report it as SPAM
B. Report it as SPAM
C. Report it as SPAM
D. Report it as SPAM

Chapter 7

- **EXERCISE:** If you completed the last exercise, your account should be set up. If not, now would be a good time to do that since we'll be building up your virtual shop throughout the rest of this book.

For a review of listing basics, go back to chapter three.

Once you have created your first listings, start engaging within the Poshmark community.

- o **Share** your items and listings on a regular basis. Don't just let them sit there. Try to do this at least once a day, if not a couple times a week.
- o **Follow** people who engage with you and your store with likes, shares, and comments.

      o **Reciprocate:** if someone shares your item, share one or more of theirs.

      o **Communicate:** if someone posts a question, it means they're interested. Respond in a timely manner.

      o **Attend Poshmark Parties:** these are great opportunities to showcase your listings and connect with potential buyers. We'll cover parties in greater detail in a separate chapter.

Chapter 8

- **EXERCISE ("Practice Gratitude"):** When you land your first sale, take a moment to savor the feeling and really understand what this means. Someone is trusting you to fulfill a need. For us, it was a pair of blue jeans. With each subsequent sale, remember the rush, the excitement, and appreciation you felt with your first sale. Pack and ship each item with care, knowing that your customer is excited to receive something that they will wear for a wedding, special occasion, job interview, holiday party, or first date.

Chapter 9

- **EXERCISE 1: The ZOA exercise.** Develop your negotiating muscles. We're going to build off the exercises we did in chapter five with more detailed information. Take two or three of your listings and figure out the **ZOA** for each. The ZOAs have two lines to write in ballpark figures.

Item	
• Original price	
• Age and Condition	
Pricing	
• Original price (max satisfaction)	
• Sell price (optimal satisfaction)	
Upper bound	
• ZOA	
• ZOA	
Lower bound	

Item	
• Original price	
• Age and Condition	
Pricing	
• Original price (max satisfaction)	
• Sell price (optimal satisfaction)	
Upper bound	
• ZOA	
• ZOA	
Lower bound	

Item	
• Original price	
• Age and Condition	
Pricing	
• Original price (max satisfaction)	
• Sell price (optimal satisfaction)	
Upper bound	
• ZOA	
• ZOA	
Lower bound	

◢ **EXERCISE 2: The negotiation simulation.** Below you'll be simulating a negotiation based on a listing with a price and specific conditions. Each choice will lead you to an outcome. Review the item, its condition, and pricing information.

    o   **Item:** a leather jacket / **Original price:** $800 / **Age and condition:** five years, has some creases and a few frays in the lining but otherwise in excellent shape / **List price:** $600.

    o   **Offer:** $300, IF you:

1. **Accept** go to 2. **Counter** go to 3. **Decline** go to 4.

2. Congrats! You sold the jacket for $300. Your earnings come to $240. Later that day, a friend asks if you still have the jacket and is willing to pay $350 for it. Write down how you feel and any thoughts or takeaways.

    _____

3. The offeror declines. You don't get any new offers and the jacket stays listed for a while. Write down how you feel and any thoughts or takeaways

    _____

5. The offeror comes back with a $330 counteroffer, IF you:
   - **Accept** go to 5. **Decline** go to 6.

6. Congrats! You closed the sale. Write down how you feel and any thoughts or takeaways.

    _____

7. The jacket doesn't sell and stays up there for a while. Write down how you feel and any thoughts or takeaways.

    _____

Confused? There is no "right" or "wrong" answer. Negotiating is an imperfect science, and everyone will have a different outcome depending on their choices. The point of this exercise is to better gauge your satisfaction levels as a seller. Understanding this will help you make better decisions as you engage in sales and negotiating offers.

Reminder: as mentioned in chapter eight, Poshmark has recently added a "match buyer's last offer" enhancement to counteroffers or what I call a "boomerang" option. Once you counter an offer, if you change your mind, you can replace it with a new one that matches the buyer's last offer.

Chapter 10

- **EXERCISE:** As you continue listing and sharing items, make sure you are replying to questions in a timely manner. If you're doing Poshmark as a side-hustle, do a time audit of your schedule to identify pockets of time to allocate to it. You may also want to find out where your nearest post office is and take a visit: see if they have an after-hours drop off slot or ask if your regular mail carrier is willing to pick up packages. Introduce yourself and be nice!

Chapter 11

- **EXERCISE:** As you continue building your store and increasing your listings, study the different buttons and interactions. If you're using Poshmark to buy as well as sell, start looking, liking, and bundling items you may want to buy. Share items when someone shares yours or be proactive and share someone else's listings if you want to show them a little love. Answer questions and establish policies and communication protocols for your store. You can do this on the "Meet your Posher" post, which is standard for all accounts. You can also create a separate post with graphics on platforms like Canva (see Figure 11.5).

THE POSHMARK GUIDE FOR INDIVIDUALS AND SMALL BUSINESSES

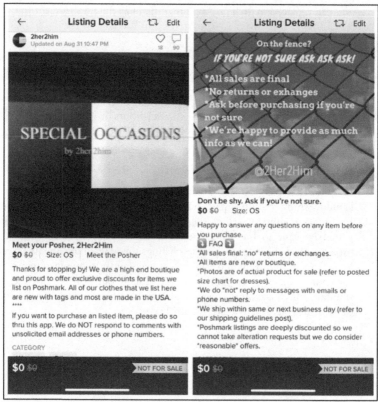

Figure 11.5 Examples of policies and protocol posts.

Chapter 12

• **EXERCISE:** Map out your day. If you're juggling a fulltime job or other responsibilities, identify pockets of time to keep active on Poshmark. It only takes a few minutes. If you're tight on time, prioritize answering questions and attending one or two Poshmark parties a week.

Chapter 13

• **EXERCISE:** If you haven't already, attend your first Poshmark party. Share your items, then go back and reciprocate follows, likes and shares. You may want to visit the virtual Poshmark showrooms, including the "party room" and "host picks," to see what kind of items are being shared and are trending. Next, look at the Poshmark ambassador and ambassador II requirements. If you've already started selling, see how far along you are. Don't worry if you have a long way to go. Focus on providing a great experience for your followers and potential buyers. You'll automatically make progress towards hitting those benchmarks.

Chapter 14

🔹 **EXERCISE:** Develop your inventory management system whether it's checkmarks on the tag or your own numbering system (especially if there is no tag). Even if you only have a few items, get into the habit early. You'll save yourself a lot of time and headache later on if you decide to grow your business. Use Canva or another graphics tool to spruce up your store with signage. I recommend creating them in advance, especially for sales, vacations, holidays, closure periods, and FAQs. Keep them on your phone and post when needed. Below are some examples of signs I've created for our store. Feel free to crib the verbiage and / or modify.

Figure 14.3 Examples of signage created on Canva.

Chapter 15

🔹 **EXERCISE:** Explore the administrative features, including "My Seller Tools" and "Notifications." Check out the "My Shoppers" section to see if there are any engagement opportunities with potential buyers. Explore "My Closet Insights" to get a big picture of how your closet is doing. Manage your store, generate a sales report, and try out the different analytic and CRM options. These will become more important as you grow your business.

Chapter 16

🔹 **EXERCISE:** If you're thinking about taking on a Poshmark partner, figure out the logistics and day-to-day responsibilities. Have the hard conversations before you enter into that partnership. How do you handle disagreements and conflicts? How do you divide responsibilities, how do you allocate your time (how much time do you have to allocate)? What do you do if things go south, and you decide to part ways? What's your exit strategy? Finally, figure out how to divide the responsibilities and rewards. Consider all of these issues before you decide to take that Posh leap together. If both of you are investing significant resources, including inventory or capital to purchase inventory, you may want to sign a formal partnership agreement. In that case, it may be a good idea for you to draft one or consult with an attorney(s).

o If you are the owner of a retail business or boutique, map out the responsibilities between you and any co-owners. Determine how you will manage your Poshmark inventory with your in-store items. Decide how you will involve sales staff in helping you run the Poshmark part of the business.

Chapter 17

● **EXERCISE:** Check out the "love notes" located inside the profiles of different Poshmark sellers. If you've started selling and are receiving reviews and ratings, look at your own. Get an idea of benchmarks and milestones to achieve, including faster shipping time to increase your ratings average.

Chapter 18

● **EXERCISE:** Go back to your exercise from chapter one. Now, think ahead to a future time, be it one year, two years, or more and write out your Poshmark goal(s) for the future.

_____

_____

_____

_____

_____

Chapter 19

● **EXERCISE:** Check out some other platforms. Do some research and see what the pros and cons are of each. If you're feeling adventurous, open an account on one or two or more and try them out. Compare and contrast your experience with Poshmark.

APPENDIX 2: QUICK REFERENCE SHEET

- **Getting Started**
  - Create your account
  - Brand your account
- **Safety**
  - Engage in app only
  - Exception: in-person customer leads for brick-and-mortar stores
- **Listing Basics**
  - Photos
  - Video
  - Title
  - Description
  - Category
  - Quantity
  - Size
  - Brand
  - Color
  - New With Tags
  - Original Price
  - Listing Price
    - Your earnings (when sold)
- **Be Proactive**
  - Like
  - Follow
  - Share
  - Create Stories
- **Pricing**
  - Salvage value for older items
  - Profit margin for new or wholesale items
- **Sales and Transactions**
  - Buy Now
  - Offers
    - Accept
    - Counter
    - Decline
  - Preparing sold items
    - Identify the item
    - Check condition
    - Take proof photos before packing
    - Pack and print label (cross-check to ensure correct)
    - Ship (wait three hours for items sold at full price)
    - Confirm on Poshmark
  - Post sales
    - Three-day inspection period
    - Accept

- Case
- **Negotiating on Poshmark**
  - Max satisfaction
  - Optimal satisfaction
  - Zone of Agreement
    - Upper Bound
    - Lower Bound
- **Interactions**
  - Likes
  - Bundles
  - Comments
  - Shares / Bulk Shares
  - Sales
- **Poshmark Parties**
  - Theme
  - General
- **Inventory Management**
  - SKUs
  - Check marks
  - Photos
- **Administrative Tools**
  - Drafts
  - Styling
  - Administrative Tools
    - My Seller Tools
    - My Shoppers
    - My Closet Insights

APPENDIX 3: INVENTORY MANAGEMENT SHEET

ITEM	
BRAND	
CONDITION	
SKU	
COLOR	
QUANTITY	
ORIGINAL PRICE	
LISTING PRICE	

ITEM	
BRAND	
CONDITION	
SKU	
COLOR	
QUANTITY	
ORIGINAL PRICE	
LISTING PRICE	

APPENDIX 4: NEGOTIATION WORKSHEET

ITEM	
AGE & CONDITION	
ORIGINAL PRICE (MAX SATISFACTION)	
SALE PRICE (OPTIMAL)	
UPPER BOUND	
ZONE OF AGREEMENT (ZOA)	
ZONE OF AGREEMENT (ZOA)	
LOWER BOUND	

ITEM	
AGE & CONDITION	
ORIGINAL PRICE (MAX SATISFACTION)	
SALE PRICE (OPTIMAL)	
UPPER BOUND	
ZONE OF AGREEMENT (ZOA)	
ZONE OF AGREEMENT (ZOA)	
LOWER BOUND	

REFERENCES AND NOTES

[1] Lambert, L. and Sraders, A. (2020, September 28). *Nearly 100,000 establishments that temporarily shut down due to the pandemic are now out of business.* Fortune. https://fortune.com/2020/09/28/covid-buisnesses-shut-down-closed/, Schweitzer, A. (2021, March 20). *Pandemic A Blow To D.C. Small Businesses, Data Show.* NPR. https://www.npr.org/2021/03/20/979594968/covid-s-toll-on-business-1.

[2] Altable, C.S., Gonzalo, A., Harreis, H., Villepelet, C. (2020, May 6). *Fashion's digital transformation: Now or never.* McKinsey. https://www.mckinsey.com/industries/retail/our-insights/fashions-digital-transformation-now-or-never, Deschamps, T. (2021, January 10), CTV News. https://www.ctvnews.ca/business/not-as-easy-as-it-looks-small-businesses-share-what-it-takes-to-move-online-1.5260897.

[3] Altable, C.S., Gonzalo, A., Harreis, H., Villepelet, C. (2020, May 6). *Fashion's digital transformation: Now or never.* McKinsey. https://www.mckinsey.com/industries/retail/our-insights/fashions-digital-transformation-now-or-never, Deschamps, T. (2021, January 10).

[4] Rogers, K. (1978). *The Gambler* [The Gambler]. United Artists.

[5] The original acronym was FOMOOP or "Fear of Missing Out on Poshmark." Credit to my editor Megan Prikhodko who suggested this snappier, easier to remember version.

[6] The technical phrase used in negotiations is "Zone of Possible Agreement" or ZOPA. For our purposes, I'm using a truncated version of the acronym and a simplified explanation of the concept. For a more technical explanation, see Merino, M. (2017, September 14). *Understanding ZOPA: The Zone of Possible Agreement.* Harvard Business School Online. https://online.hbs.edu/blog/post/understanding-zopa.

[7] Constable, K. (2022, August 11). *15 Side Hustles That Still Make Money in 2022, According to People Who Do Them Every Day.* NextAdvisor. https://time.com/nextadvisor/financial-independence/best-side-hustles.

[8] Disclaimer: This book does not give tax advice. For classification or reporting questions, please consult with a tax professional.

[9] Obviously, we didn't escalate this example!

[10] Chen, C. (2021, January 17). *A Poshmark seller nabbed over $12,000 by buying stock in the company's successful IPO. Here's how she did it.* Insider. https://www.businessinsider.com/a-poshmark-seller-nabbed-12000-by-buying-into-the-ipo-2021-1, Grigsby, C. (2020, October 19). *Dumpster-Diving Mom Makes Thousands Selling "Garbage."* Spectrum Local News. https://spectrumlocalnews.com/tx/south-texas-el-paso/news/2020/10/18/dumpster-diving-mom-makes-thousands-selling--garbage-, Locker, M. (2021, June 22). *How to Turn Your Unwanted Possessions Into Cash Online.* AARP. https://www.aarp.org/home-family/your-home/info-2021/tips-for-selling-products-online.html., Poshmark. (n.d.). *Poshmark's 2020 social commerce report.* Poshmark. https://blog.poshmark.com/2020/02/27/poshmarks-2020-social-commerce-report/, Wicker, A. (2020, December 10). WIRED. https://www.wired.com/story/get-rich-selling-used-fashion-online-or-cry-trying/.

ADDITIONAL RESOURCES

- Moving Forward Poshmark series (blogs and podcast) available at www.bemovingforward.com.
- The Poshmark Journal for Individuals and Small Businesses (available on Amazon).
    - o A journal containing blank inventory and negotiation worksheets to manage your Poshmark business.

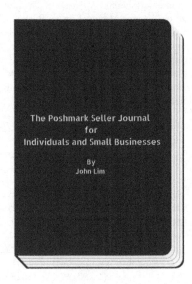

ABOUT THE AUTHOR

John Lim is the author of *The Poshmark Guide for Individuals and Small Businesses: How We Achieved a Five-Figure Revenue Stream Within Our First Year*, and creator of *Corporate Cliches: An Adult Coloring Book for Passive Aggressive Stress Relief Against Eye-Roll Inducing Office Sayings*. He is the voiceover talent for the audiobook version of the award-winning book, *I Am a Professional Metalhead*, written by Angelo Spenillo. John has been featured in *Cracked, The Baltimore Sun, Authority Magazine, Voyage LA*, and numerous podcasts. He is the executive producer and host of the Moving Forward podcast series, which has reached listeners across the U.S., and in over 50 countries.

John is a former actor for television and film, having acted in productions for The National Geographic Channel, The History Channel, and HBO Productions. He is known to many sci-fi fans for his role as "Young Lt. Cmdr. Sulu," opposite legendary actor George Takei in the production of *Star Trek: World and Enough and Time*, written by Emmy Award™ winning screenwriter, Michael Reeves. John's performance captured the attention of top Hollywood Casting Director, April Webster, and led to an audition for a co-starring role in the feature film, Star Trek (2009), directed by JJ Abrams.

John is a 2018 TEDx speaker and earned his BA from The University of Pennsylvania, his JD from Georgetown Law, and his MBA from The Johns Hopkins University Carey Business School.

Made in the USA
Las Vegas, NV
26 October 2023

79742363R00108